Equity in the Workplace
Stories from Black Irish Women in Ireland

Equity in the Workplace
Stories from Black Irish Women in Ireland

Edited by Dr Ebun Joseph

Copyright © Ebun Joseph, 2024

First Published in Ireland, in 2024, in co-operation with
Choice Publishing, Drogheda, County Louth, Republic of Ireland.
www.choicepublishing.ie
Paperback ISBN: 978-1-913275-97-6

All rights reserved. No part of this publication may be reproduced, stored in a retrieval system, transmitted in any form, or by any means, electronic, mechanical, photocopying, recording or otherwise, without the prior permission of the copyright holder.

Cover photo by Ebun Joseph

This anthology *Equity in the workplace: Stories from Black Irish women in Ireland*, provides readers the opportunity to gain insider glimpses of what it is to be a Black Irish woman working in Ireland in the 21st century. The plurality of multigenerational insights of the contributors is a real plus of the book, as are the varied workplace experiences they highlight. What emerges across the chapters are the voices of people who are strong within themselves, their identities, and professional expertise and emboldened by the writing process to articulate the ways in which they are all too often constrained because of the discrimination they endure as Black and African women. They echo many of us when they express their disappointment about the continued inequalities across Irish society because, in part, they also hope for change.

Prof. Dina Zoe Belluigi
Queen's University Belfast

This book is an essential read for any individual or organisation interested in achieving equity in the Irish labour market. It's insightful exploration of inequity in the labour market through compelling narratives of the lived experiences of 15 women and 1 man from diverse backgrounds, sheds light on the persistent challenges Black Irish women face in the Irish labour market, and offers valuable insights for how we can create a more equitable workplace. This book also provides practical strategies to address systemic inequalities, empowering individuals and organisations to create a more inclusive and fair workplace for all. I recommend this book as a tool for better understanding and advocating for equity in the labour market, with practical solutions for addressing systemic disparities. It is a must-have resource for anyone committed to fostering inclusive workplaces and promoting economic justice.

Yemi Adenuga
Director of Programs- MiB Institute of People Development

As a Mincéir (Irish Traveller) woman, I have witnessed and experienced many incidents of discrimination both within the workplace and in Irish society in general. In this book, Ebun Joseph has respectfully brought together the heartfelt stories and experiences of Black Irish women in the workplace while providing the reader with tangible guidelines on how to tackle workplace inequity. Filled with wisdom and insight on the issues of racism, discrimination, inequality and exclusion, this book offers a thoughtful look at intersectionality through the words and voices of Black Irish women which give a compelling backdrop to the experiences of minority ethnic groups in Ireland. Ebun's book confronts the systems of power and power relations in the workplace. It is a timely guide needed to bring about systematic and institutional change to make the workplace more equal and equitable for all.

Dr Sindy Joyce,
Sociologist, University of Limerick
Member of President Michael D Higgins Council of State.

Equity in the workplace: Stories from Black Irish women in Ireland is a critical examination of the challenges Black Irish women face in achieving workplace equity. The book delves into the historical oppression, discrimination, and systemic racism that have marginalised Black women, emphasising the intersection of gender-based discrimination and racism. It highlights the underrepresentation of Black Irish women in leadership roles, attributing this to racial and gender identity as well as to Ireland's practices of equity and equality. The authors explores the concepts of equity versus equality, proposing an innovative approach: equality of experience, aimed at ensuring the same quality of experience for all within systems, organisations, or society. This book is a call to action for inclusive policies and actions to address the disparities rooted in race and gender, advocating for systemic change to genuinely promote equity in the workplace.

Cllr. Lilian Seenoi Barr
Founder and Director, North West Migrants Forum,
Londonderry, Northern Ireland
Elected representative, Derry City & Strabane District Council

Equity in the workplace: Stories from Black Irish women in Ireland is a really significant piece of writing. It has opened my eyes further to the plight of Black Irish women, particularly in the workplace. It shines a light on the stark differences Black Irish women must face in challenging sexist views as women and racist treatment as Black people. Their different treatment compared to White women and to Black men is laid bare in the stories shared by these brave authors. Dr Ebun Joseph and the Unforgettable Women's Network have created something really special and important here. I would go so far as to say it should be read and understood by everyone entering the workforce in Ireland today; our leaders, managers, recruiters, and human resource professionals need to read it.

Leon Diop
CEO, Black and Irish

Foreword

Orla O'Connor
Director, National Women's Council

I was so pleased to be asked to give the foreword for this timely and skilfully curated book. Black Irish women have made rich and vibrant contributions to so many aspects of Irish life, and particularly the Irish feminist movement. Without the constant and active amplification of Black women's voices and experiences, there can be no true progress towards women's equality.

This book is an essential document in how it sets out the myriad of additional barriers that Black women face in the workplace: the microaggressions, the profiling, the pay disparity, the prejudice against 'non-Irish' names to name but a few. Taking the issue of pay alone – it's well documented that the gender pay gap and gender pension gap is exacerbated by racism and discrimination. From our research, and from the testimonies in this book, we know that Black women experience extremely high rates of discrimination both looking for work and, in the workplace, compared to White Irish nationals. Migrant women are at greater risk of exploitation, with 44% of participants in one study reporting that they received less than the minimum wage. While racism affects both men and women, women experience both racism *and* sexism, and Black women are more likely to be affected. This is why an intersectional approach, one that leaves no woman behind, is so critical to any feminist advocacy work.

Racism is a key barrier to increasing the diversity and representativeness of our political leaders. In *Women Beyond the Dáil*, a National Women's Council's 2019 report, local political discourse where, for example, rhetoric used to resist allocation of Traveller accommodation uses stereotypes that demean Traveller experiences. Discrimination against Irish Travellers is nothing new in this country and it obviously extends to all minoritised groups, including Black women. While there has been some progress in political representation – for example, the 2021 election of Uruemu Adejinmi as Ireland's first Black woman mayor – the rate of change is simply too slow.

In a representative democracy, it matters who represents us. The research indicates a clearer and more consistent interest in social issues, for instance more women than men are reporting issues such as poverty and racism as priority issues. The continued low numbers of women in local government means that women have less access to power, and this causes deficits in the quality of local democracy. The single, most important and effective measure we can take is to implement a gender quota for local and national elections. As Eya Lawani outlines in her piece, affirmative action is a hugely effective route to equity, both in the labour market and in politics.

Visibility is vital. And as Emer O'Neill references in her contribution, "if you can't be it, you can't see it". The most challenging part of this maxim is that, for women, with greater visibility comes great vulnerability to abuse and harassment online. And because Black women face multiple layers of discrimination, they are also more vulnerable when visible in an online space. We know that minority ethnic women are one of the most targeted and trolled groups on social media platforms. In Ireland, this toxic behaviour (i.e., hostility, harassment, and hate) acts as a deterrent to women in putting themselves forward for election and in so many other realms. This issue must be tackled urgently so that women in all professional spheres – politicians, entrepreneurs, journalists, activists etc. – can navigate the online space without fear.

In Ireland, we're increasingly seeing how the growing far right movement threatens democracy. We must take racism and discrimination very seriously and expose and challenge far right ideology where it is disguised as 'free speech' and the voice of a 'silenced majority'. We must all be willing to continuously reflect on our own actions and challenge our own prejudice and unconscious bias to better understand the connection between sexism, racism, and other forms of discrimination. Intersectional feminism, one that includes the voices of Black and other minoritised women at its core, is the only path toward true equality.

Preface

To amplify the voices of Black Irish women, this book examines their experiences within the Irish labour market. It aims to uncover the challenges they face and their perceptions of achieving equity in the workplace. Despite progress in gender parity, disparities still exist, with women being underrepresented in leadership roles and facing lower pay, poor working conditions, and instances of bullying and harassment. Black women often face more obstacles in achieving equity. In response to the "Embracing Equity" theme of International Women's Day in March 2023, the Institute of Anti-racism and Black Studies partnered with the Unforgettable Women's Network and 10 Black Irish women professionals to explore gender equity for Black women in the workforce. Through a documentary that included insights from White Irish academics and allies, the discussion around equity in the workplace was expanded. This book project involved collaboration with additional authors to provide a comprehensive view of the experiences of Black Irish women in different sectors and age groups. The resulting collection of 16 chapters is a resource for understanding and addressing the gender bias, stereotypes, emotional labour, and challenges faced by Black Irish women in the labour market in 2024. It sheds light on the efforts made by these women to achieve equity, emphasizing the importance of collective activism, sponsorship, social capital, allyship, solidarity and acceptance. By sharing personal journeys and perspectives, this book aims to promote equal opportunities for all individuals in the workplace and advocates for the positive representation of Black Irish women in society. It suggests four key strategies for attaining equity: (i) the practice of equality of experience, (ii) integrating acceptance of difference into all workplace practices, (iii) the provision of safe spaces for interaction and healing, and (iv) a labour market leadership activation and strategic plan for Black Irish women. We are indebted to the authors who contributed to this book; their dedication and openness in sharing their stories have generated a broader dialogue on gender equity and inclusion in the Irish workforce – long overdue in Ireland in 2024.

Ebun Joseph is CEO and founder of The Institute of Anti-racism and Black Studies (www.iabs.ie). She is the Coordinator and lecturer of the first Black Studies & Critical Race Theory module in Ireland, at the School of Education, University College Dublin, Ireland

Acknowledgements

This book would not have been possible without the contributions of the Black Irish women who partnered with me and openly shared their unique stories and insights here and in a 2023 TV documentary. I am indebted to the authors for their stories which have generated a broader dialogue on gender equity and inclusion in the Irish workforce. Your talent, dedication, and unique voices have brought this book to life in ways I could never have imagined. The documentary and this book are a testament to their desire to see positive change in Ireland. A special thank you to my children Alex and Patrick for their continued support and understanding. Your love and encouragement keeps me going, thank you! Special thanks to Anne Downes for copy-editing and proofreading the text. I am also grateful to Danielle Mogere, our project worker, for her supportive work. My biggest gratitude is always to God for the grace to surpass my own strength. This project was made possible through funding from Community Foundation Ireland. We are deeply appreciative. Thank you to everyone who played a part in bringing this book to fruition. Your collective efforts have created something truly special, and I am forever grateful.

Contents

List of Contributors	xiv
Introduction.	xix
Dr Ebun Joseph	

1. Embracing diversity — 1
Dr Ebun Joseph
CEO & founder, Institute of Anti-racism and Black Studies
Coordinator and lecturer of the first Black Studies & Critical Race Theory module in Ireland

2. Equity continues to evade Black Irish women in the workplace — 11
Carline Thompson-Kelly
Nurse, Researcher, Author, and Activist

3. Barriers to gaining equity for Black Irish women — 19
Melissa Bosch,
Head of Diversity, Equity, and Inclusion, EY Ireland

4. Unconscious bias affects equity for Black Irish women in the labour market — 29
Emer O'Neill
Teacher, author, broadcaster and public speaker

5. Is the lack of equity for Black Irish women intentional? — 35
Tafadzwa Mandiwanza
Consultant paediatric neurosurgeon

6. Black Irish women are denied equity within the workplace — 41
Dr. Phil Mullen
Assistant Professor of Black Studies

7. Discrimination and negative attitudes towards Black Irish women maintain inequity — 49
Dr Salome Mbugua
CEO of AkiDwA, The Migrant Women's Network Ireland

8. Black women in Irish society are the 'other' — 54
Winifred Ikhine Akinyemi
Civil servant, Department of Foreign Affairs

Contents

9. Equity doesn't play well for the Black Irish woman; it hasn't worked for me   61
Dr Loveth Owhor
Medical researcher and bioresource technologist

10. Equitable work environments should remove barriers   66
Grace Oladipo
Desk Officer, Department of Foreign Affairs

11. Black Irish women and equity in the workplace   73
Ellie Kisyombe
Founder, 'Ellie's Kitchen Home Edition', political aspirant, activist

12. Women of African descent face racial and gender bias at work   76
Sola Mobolaji
Senior Social Worker

13. A double disadvantage not just as women, but as Black women   82
Eya Lawani
SNA and Social Justice Advocate

14. Black Irish women carry a double burden   89
Kathleen Lynch
Professor of Equality Studies Emerita, University College Dublin.
Senior Lectureship (Associate Professorship) in Education.
Commissioner with the Irish Human Rights and Equality Commission (IHREC)

15. Seeing the human as the human is not as we want them to be   98
Dr. Mel Duffy
Lecturer, Sociology and Sexuality Studies
Dublin City University

16. Accepting, valuing and supporting Black Irish women in place-making in Ireland   105
Dr Ebun Joseph, CEO & founder, Institute of Anti-racism and Black Studies
Professor Emerita Kathleen Lynch, UCD Equality Studies
Senator Tom Clonan, Member of Seanad Éireann

List of Contributors

Dr Ebun Joseph is a diversity and race relations consultant, CEO & founder, of the Institute of Anti-racism and Black Studies (IABS), and coordinator and lecturer of the Black Studies module at University College Dublin (UCD). She is also the founder & chairperson of the African Scholars Association Ireland, AFSAI (2018-2022). Dr Joseph held the position of Career Development Consultant at the Royal College of Surgeons in Ireland (2017-2021), and was a Teaching Fellow at Trinity College Dublin, Training and Employment Officer EPIC (2007-2017). Ebun is an author, TV panellist, columnist and an equality activist. With a research focus on labour markets and race relations, she has presented at many business and NGO conferences. Ebun is a published author and contributes regular responses on contemporary issues of race and racism in Ireland. Her book is *Racial Stratification in Ireland: A Critical Race Theory of Labour Market Inequality*. She also co-authored the book, *Challenging Perceptions of Africa in Schools: Critical Approaches to Global Justice Education*. Dr Joseph's 2020 article won the IRJ Prize awarded to the paper adjudicated to represent the best original contribution to the journal in a given year. *'Composite counter storytelling as a technique for challenging ambivalence about race and racism in the labour market in Ireland.'*

Carline Thompson is a nurse, researcher, entrepreneur, author, and activist. She hails from a small island in the Caribbean Sea called Jamaica. She is a three-time alumni member of Trinity College Dublin (TCD). She graduated with both first and second-class honours. Her academic achievement includes a BSc in intellectual disability nursing, an MSc in disability studies, and an MSc in healthcare management. Her research interests incorporate racial discrimination, ethnic minorities studies, racial trauma, intellectual disabilities, dementia, social justice, and health and well-being. She is the owner of Jam-Ire, a home baking and pastry business that introduces a taste of Jamaica with an Irish twist. She has recently co-authored a book *Building our Network*. She is also an active member of several committees and community organisations here in Ireland.

Ellie Kisyombe is a Malawian activist and multi-faceted force for change, embodying activism, entrepreneurship, and maternal strength. As co-founder of 'Our Table', she champions the economic empowerment of asylum seekers, refugees, and immigrants through social enterprise. Ellie's dedication to breaking barriers earned her recognition as 'Mum of the Year for 2022' by *Woman's Way* & Beko, celebrating her tireless efforts in the campaign to abolish direct provision. A skilled chef, she brings culinary excellence to her latest venture, Ellie's Kitchen Home Edition, merging her passion for food with her commitment to community upliftment. With each endeavour, Ellie exemplifies resilience, compassion, and leadership, inspiring others to strive for a more just and inclusive society. Her journey reflects the power of individuals to affect meaningful change, one dish, one policy, one heart at a time.

Emer O'Neill is a seasoned moderator, host, presenter and public speaker with vast experience in the areas of sustainability, global citizenship, anti-racism, inclusion and equity, women/girls in sport, children and youth education and mental health advocacy. She is a mother of three with a BA in Education and a master's in Educational Leadership and Administration with 15 years of teaching experience. She is a retired professional Irish International Basketball player and a former recipient of a scholarship to the USA to play basketball. Emer is an advocate for promoting a positive body image and self-love. She presents 'Keep It Up', a TV show that investigates why 12-14-year-old girls often drop out of sport in Ireland. It is a 6-part documentary series available on the RTE Player. Emer is the author of a *The Same but Different,* a story about a little girl overcoming her self-doubt and her journey to embrace her differences and uniqueness.

Eya Lawani is a special needs assistant (SNA) who has worked in the educational sector for over 17 years. Passionate about youth justice and keeping young people out of the criminal justice system, she has worked in both paid and voluntary roles to ensure that young people are supported to reach their potential. She holds a BA in political science from her home country of Nigeria, and a postgraduate diploma in conflict and dispute resolution from TCD. Eya is passionate about education and justice, and advocates for vulnerable groups like young Black boys who are at risk of becoming stereotyped and excluded from mainstream society, as well as her young students whose learning disabilities present an excluding barrier in a world which values a different kind of ability. The need to advocate for equality and inclusion further led Eya to continue her studies for a master's degree in Equality Studies at University College Dublin's School of Social Policy and Law. As a first generation Irish migrant woman, Eya has lived in Ireland for 24 years and is raising a young family. She is interested in Critical Race studies and fascinated by the power of

List of contributors

reframing and counter story telling in challenging inequality. The hope of building brave, safe and transformational spaces, where everyone is equally valued in a welcoming and more inclusive Ireland which embraces differences, is Eya's hope for Ireland.

Grace Oladipo is a distinguished Nigerian-Irish social entrepreneur and human rights educator. She earned her law degree from UCD in 2020, achieving notable distinctions such as the UCD President's Award, the Unilever Individual Purpose Award, and the Arthur Cox Contribution to University Life Award. She obtained an LL.M in International Human Rights Law as a Fulbright Scholar at the University of Notre Dame, Indiana, USA where she received the Faculty Award for Excellence in International Law. Grace also enriched her expertise at The Hague Academy of International Law and at the Office of the High Commissioner for Human Rights in Geneva before assuming her current role as a Desk Officer at the Department of Foreign Affairs. Passionate about empowering women, Grace founded AudacityXX, an organisation dedicated to helping females overcome professional barriers. Her extensive international experiences over the past 6 years, spanning five countries, fuels her commitment to driving positive change.

Professor Kathleen Lynch is an emerita professor of equality studies at UCD and a serving member of the Irish Human Rights and Equality Commission (IHREC). She has worked over many years to promote equality and social justice through research, education, and activism. A visiting scholar in many of the world's leading universities, she has authored several books and articles on all types of equality and social justice issues, especially on education, and, more recently, on care and social justice. Her most recent book, *Care and Capitalism: Why Affective Equality Matters for Social Justice,* was published by Polity Press, Cambridge in 2022. Her forthcoming book, *A Critique of Human Capital in Education* will be published in 2025 by Routledge. She was awarded the *UCD Medal for Pioneering Change,* in 2018, and the Irish Research Council, *President of Ireland Prize* for her work in promoting Equality and Social Justice, in 2019.

Dr. Loveth Owhor is a bioresource technologist and medical researcher. Her area of research is in reproductive medicine, specialising on the female reproductive system where she investigates inflammation in the fallopian tubes utilising novel live cell imaging. Her research work has been published by *Nature Scientific Reports* journal. She has over 11 years' experience of working in both the academic and healthcare sectors. She holds an MSc in bioresource technology and a PhD in medicine from UCD School of Agriculture & Food Science and UCD School of Medicine, respectively. Dr. Owhor is also a presenter on the Introduction to Black Studies module, which is taught in the Institute of Anti-racism and Black Studies where she unveils the untold stories about Africa with her lesson on 'Africa and Africans' contributions to science, medicine and agriculture'. Dr. Owhor is Secretary of the African Scholars Association Ireland (AFSAI) and Company Secretary of the Institute of Anti-racism and Black Studies (IABS).

Dr. Mel Duffy is Assistant Professor in the School of Nursing & Human Sciences, Dublin City University (DCU). She is a recognized international expert in hermeneutic phenomenological (HP) research across the health and social sciences. Her research seeks to identify pathways to investigate hidden populations and bring forth their voices to society. For example, the recently completed research project 'Mapping the Lived Experience of Intersex/Variations of Sex Characteristics in Ireland: Contextualising Lay and Professional Knowledge to Enable Development of Appropriate Law and Policy (2022)' is the first study of its kind in Ireland that sheds light on what it means to be born intersex i.e., with a variation in one's sex characteristics.

Melissa Bosch is Head of Diversity, Equity, and Inclusion (DE&I) at EY Ireland. She is an accomplished diversity, equity, and inclusion strategist with a proven track record in driving innovative and strategic interventions for various organisations. She is known for her behavioural change and social justice interventions, which focus on unlocking individual, societal, and organisational potential. She was brought up in South Africa and her ethos is seeded in the African philosophy of 'Ubuntu' and the belief that incredible things happen when people are seen, valued, empowered, and involved. With this deep-rooted passion for fostering inclusive cultures, her approach to DE&I has consistently triggered meaningful change. Melissa's commitment and ingenuity in the field of DE&I have won her numerous accolades. These awards re-affirmed her understanding of the unique interplay between individuality, organisational culture, and societal pressures. Beyond her professional achievements, Melissa is a fervent advocate for social justice through her charity and volunteer work. She holds a master's of business degree in equality, diversity, and inclusion.

List of contributors

Dr. Philomena Mullen is Assistant Professor of Black Studies in the Department of Sociology, TCD. She completed a PhD as a Government of Ireland PhD scholar; she studied the racialised experiences of Black mixed African-Irish women in Ireland's industrial school system and their construction of identity in a White society. She is co-chair of the Race, Ethnicity and Equality Working Group in TCD and is a member of the Advisory Board of TCD's Colonial Legacies project. She is a Trustee of the Association of Mixed-Race Irish (AMRI), and a member of African Scholars Association of Ireland (AFSAI). She is also a member of the UN International Decade for People of African Descent Ireland Steering Committee 2015-2024. Her research interests include racialisation processes and recovering the historical presence of Africans in Ireland and in the institutional care system in 1940-1980 Ireland.

Dr. Salome Mbugua, is a researcher, gender equality activist, human rights advocate, and the founder and CEO of AkiDwA (sisterhood in Swahili), the migrant women's network in Ireland. She was appointed as Commissioner in the Irish Human Rights and Equality Commission by President Michael D. Higgins in 2016. With over 20 years of professional experience, Dr. Mbugua has dedicated her career to working in civil society, focusing on supporting underrepresented groups, particularly women, children, and youth, in Europe and Africa. Her profound belief in equality and justice has not only shaped her career but has driven her engagement with policymakers at national, European, and international levels. Dr. Mbugua is actively involved in various advisory committees, expert groups, and boards across Ireland and Europe. She sits on the EU Expert Group on Economic Migration and chairs the working group responsible for developing Ireland's 3rd National Action Plan on Women, Peace, and Security. She also serves as an independent chair of the Equality, Diversity & Inclusion Advisory Board in the Public Appointment Service. Dr. Mbugua's accolades include being a 2015 OHCHR-UN Fellow and a 2010 Eisenhower Fellow. Dr. Mbugua earned her PhD from TCD and holds a master's degree from UCD.

Sola Mobolaji is a Coru registered senior social worker with a primary /postgraduate degree in education and a master's degree in social science (social work) from University College Dublin. For over 30 years, Sola has had a range of work experiences in different areas. She worked as a teacher. Sola has experience of working with vulnerable people using an anti-oppressive framework. Sola worked for the Health Service Executive (HSE) with women in prostitution and women who have been sex trafficked. She completed assessments, advocated, contributed to research, delivered lectures, and engaged in direct work with women from a trauma informed perspective. She works in a voluntary capacity mediating, advocating, supporting, and acting as a bridge for families that are struggling with parenting their children and those struggling with engaging with child protection services. Sola is passionate about using her skills and knowledge to support the vulnerable in society to maximise their potential.

Ms Tafadzwa Mandiwanza is a paediatric neurosurgeon who was born and raised in Zimbabwe. She completed her undergraduate medical degree at UCC, Ireland before undertaking neurosurgical training in Dublin and Cork, obtaining the FRCSI (Neurosurgery). She completed a sub-specialty fellowship in Paediatric Neurosurgery at Great Ormond Street Hospital, London and works as a Consultant Neurosurgeon position at Children's Health Ireland, Temple Street. She is the first female paediatric neurosurgeon in Ireland, and she is a wife and mother to 3 children.

Senator Tom Clonan was elected to Seanad Éireann in March 2022. Tom is a fully independent senator, with no links to any political party. Tom's mission as a Trinity College Dublin senator is to hold the Government to account. Tom graduated from TCD in 1987. For over 25 years, Tom has been a tireless campaigner for the rights of others – as an Army whistleblower on gender-based violence and as a parent campaigning for the rights of disabled children, adults, and the elderly.

Winifred Ikhine Akinyemi trained as a barrister and solicitor in Nigeria. After moving to Ireland 20 years ago in 2004, (when her law degree was not recognized in Ireland), she retrained and obtained a bachelor's degree in international development from Kimmage Development Studies Centre – now part of Maynooth University. She also holds a master's degree in international development from UCD. Winifred is an Irish civil servant working in the Department of Foreign Affairs (DFA). Since joining the Department in 2012, she has contributed to the implementation of Ireland's International Development Policy and Diaspora policy. Winifred contributes to the DFA's Gender Equality Diversity and Inclusion initiative and she is the Chairperson of the Multicultural Working Group. Winifred volunteers in her local community where she is the Chairperson of the Adamstown Community Summer Camp. She is the coordinator of the Adamstown Irish History Project and Africa Day Lucan.

Introduction
Equality of experience is the minimum requirement

Dr Ebun Joseph
CEO & Founder, Institute of Anti-racism and Black Studies

Feminist efforts to politicize experiences of women and antiracist efforts to politicize experiences of 'people of colour' have frequently proceeded as though the issues and experiences they each detail occur on mutually exclusive terrains. Although racism and sexism readily intersect in the lives of real people, they seldom do in feminist and antiracist practices. And so, when the practices expound identity as 'woman' or 'person of colour' as an either/or proposition, they relegate the identity of women of colour to a location that resists telling (Crenshaw, 1991: 1242).

The experiences of Black women have been shaped by a long history of oppression, discrimination, and marginalisation. The history of enslavement and segregation, which is now felt through ongoing systemic racism, have created significant barriers for Black women and men to overcome. Organisational practices often fail to address these historical injustices and do not consider the unique circumstances faced by Black people. In the labour market in Ireland, there is no formal recognition of the need for targeted support and resources to uplift and empower Black Irish women who face a particularly complex set of challenges due to their intersecting identities of race and gender. Gender-based discrimination and racism intertwine, resulting in unique experiences that differ from those of Black men and White women. Equality measures and policies often focus solely on single issues of gender or race, neglecting the intersectional experiences of Black women. For example, in Ireland, where we have nine grounds under which we cannot discriminate, (gender, marital status, family status, age, disability, sexual orientation, race, religion, and membership of the Traveller community), the policies do not acknowledge the intersections and so they do not actively address the specific needs of Black Irish women or any other intersection.

One glaring problem in the Irish labour market is the persistent underrepresentation of Black and African Irish women across various sectors, particularly in leadership roles. This is despite their resilience, active participation in society and high level of education (Joseph, 2020). Their voices, experiences, and talents often remain sidelined, creating a significant barrier to them achieving equity. This raises a question on if the difficulty is due to their identity as Black Irish women or the ways equity and equality is practised in Ireland. Equity and equality are two terms that are often used interchangeably, but they hold distinct meanings. In the context of the experiences faced by Black Irish women, it is essential to understand the difference between equity and equality because we all do not start from the same place (Joseph, 2018). Understanding the difference between equality of outcomes and equality of opportunity is also important in this context.

Equity refers to the principle of fairness and justice in providing resources, opportunities, and treatment to individuals or groups, ensuring that everyone has access to what they need to thrive. Equity recognizes that people have different needs and levels of advantage or disadvantage. It acknowledges the historical disadvantages and systemic barriers faced by certain communities. It takes into account the specific needs and circumstances of individuals or groups. Equity is like calculating and giving a head start to a 10-year-old 5'5" person in a race with a 25-year-old person who is 6'3" in height. For the race to be fair, a reasonable allowance must be made for the relative age difference, length of legs, stage of bone development and body strength. Therefore, equitable practices involve distributing resources and opportunities in a manner that accounts for these differences, aiming to level the playing field and address systemic barriers in order to ensure that everyone has a fair chance to succeed. Ultimately, equity seeks to promote justice and inclusivity by addressing historical and systemic inequalities and fostering environments where all individuals can reach their full potential.

Equality refers to the state of being equal in rights, status, opportunities, or treatment, regardless of individual differences such as race, gender, ethnicity, socio-economic status, or other characteristics. It embodies the principle that all individuals should be treated with the same dignity, respect, and consideration under the law and in society. In the context of social justice and human rights, equality means ensuring that everyone has equal access to resources, opportunities, and protections, without discrimination or prejudice. This can include equal pay for equal work, equal access to education and healthcare, and equal treatment before the law. While equality aims to eliminate unjust disparities and promote fairness, the characteristics society, governments, businesses and employers use to select where everyone is treated the same, can sometimes be problematic for minorities and minoritized groups.

Introduction

Equality of outcomes focuses on ensuring that everyone achieves the same or similar results, regardless of their starting point, effort, or circumstances. It seeks to eliminate disparities in outcomes such as income, wealth, education attainment, employment status, and other measurable indicators of well-being. Achieving equality of outcomes often requires redistributive policies and interventions designed to level the playing field and reduce disparities between individuals or groups. We often talk about equality of outcome. This however can be more complex and dependent on many variables. While this idea may seem appealing, it can be difficult to achieve. This is because in a diverse society, people have different skills, interests, talents, drive, motivations, and family background, which makes it difficult to ensure identical outcomes for everyone. People also will not put in the same effort.

Equality of opportunity is about ensuring that everyone has an equal chance of succeeding and achieving their potential, regardless of factors such as race, gender, socio-economic status, or other characteristics. It focuses on removing barriers and obstacles that might impede individuals from accessing opportunities, such as discriminatory practices, systemic inequalities, and limited access to resources. Equality of opportunity does not guarantee equal outcomes but aims to create a fair and meritocratic system where individuals can compete on a level playing field based on their abilities and efforts. Equality of opportunity refers to a society where everyone, regardless of their background, has fair and equal access to essential resources such as education, healthcare, employment, and housing. In essence, it's about providing a level playing field for all individuals to pursue their goals and aspirations. We all deserve an equal chance to thrive.

I advocate for a third option – equality of experience – where everyone who comes into that system, who meets you, your team/department, who comes in to that organisation, who comes to work with you or uses your products, can have the same [e]quality of experience. While we often talk about equality of outcome, this however can be more complex and dependent on many variables. If we cannot achieve the minimum, which is the equality of experience, how can we attain equality of opportunity or the more complex one – equality of outcome?

When we talk about the concept of equity, we are saying that we want to ensure people have equality of experience. So, whether they are in a wheelchair, whether they wear a hijab, whether their skin colour is Black or Brown; whether they are Irish Travellers, Roma, Lithuanian, Polish, or Latvian, can we ensure we have equality of experience in the labour market? Can we operate in ways that do not create hate between groups by pitting groups against each other.

Introduction

As interesting as the concept of equity is, if I answer the question, which I want you all to answer for us, *do Black Irish women experience equity in the workplace?*, my answer would be no. I have not experienced equity in my work life in Ireland. I also don't have too many friends who have experienced equity in Ireland. Note, I have not said I am *not doing well*, I am not doing well in terms of an equitable work life experience. I *am* doing well *in spite of* the obstacles and barriers I experienced. What were these obstacles? Well, I remember applying for the same job (in another organisation) as another woman whom I had earlier mentored when she first started working with me. She was invited for the job interview and I wasn't. I think about the fact that I was not invited for a job interview as a guidance councillor in a university until I had a PhD (Level 10 Award) when the requirement for that role was a postgraduate diploma (Level 9 Award). But she was White. In fact, I got my first interview for a third level guidance councillor role after spending another 6 years in education compared to my White colleagues (4 for a PhD and 2 for a Masters).

One of the worst experiences was applying for a lecturer role and not even being shortlisted. When I asked for feedback, I learned that while I received a score of 10/10 for my degree, they scored me 5/10 for my knowledge of equality(!) Can you imagine that? This was in 2019. I had a PhD in equality studies, I had published articles and was a national voice on diversity, race, racism, and anti-racism in the labour market. It was a strange experience to find out that after 4 years I had been paying a higher rate for car hire purchase (presumably because of my skin colour); and sad for me to witness shop assistants smile patiently at other children on the queue and have a long face when it was my child's turn. Of course, not every day in Ireland is full of bad experiences, and there are good people everywhere. At the same time, we cannot sweep these experiences under the carpet if we want to see change for the next generation of Black (and White) women and men. All the Black Irish women interviewed about their experiences in work in Ireland agreed that equity certainly does not exist for Black women in the Irish labour market.

This book sets out to give voice to Black and African Irish women on their experiences of and encounters with navigating the labour market in Ireland. It sought to understand how these professional women in Ireland view their chances of accessing an equitable outcome in the workplace. Although gender parity is improving with more women on boards, and businesses being mandated to report on the gender pay gap, we know that disparity in labour market outcomes still exist. Women continue to be underrepresented in management, senior roles and as academic professors. They earn less than their male counterparts, face poorer working conditions and are more prone to bullying and harassment. Women of migrant descent in Ireland reported being assigned a gendered role with a lower pay scale (Joseph, 2020). A recent study in Ireland shows that minority women experience an even greater disparity than other women and they have a double penalty when it comes to gender parity (ESRI, 2023).

In March 2023, in response to the International Women's Day theme of embracing equity for women, the Institute of Anti-racism and Black Studies collaborated with the Unforgettable Women's Network to explore the gender equity for Black Irish women in the world of work. It raised a serious question for us on the level of equity that Black Irish women have as they make their place in Ireland. A documentary was produced where 10 professional Black Irish women leaders in Ireland discussed their experience of equity in the workplace. We spoke with women who are accomplished in community work and successful in their fields, and have been able to navigate the labour market. This exploration was supported by two White academics and allies. To include more sectors and women from the 20–29 age bracket, we asked five more authors to collaborate with the book project. The 26-minute documentary formed the impetus for this collection of stories which can be used together with the documentary. This book is suitable for students of business, development, gender, and social sciences as well as human resource professionals, EDI specialist and managers who might be interested in achieving gender parity in their businesses.

To develop this book, we asked all participants the following five questions:
- Do Black Irish women have equity in the labour market in Ireland? If yes, why do you say that; if no, why do you say that?
- What do you consider to be the problem with Black Irish women accessing equity?
- What do we need for Black Irish women to have equity?
- Most Black Irish women do extra work such as volunteering roles in society in addition to their paid work. Why do you think this is so and does this apply to you?
- Can you describe your journey to your current role?

The authors brought up a variety of issues, such as the discrimination faced by minority ethnic healthcare professionals, which Carline Thompson said had negative impact on their mental, financial, and physical well-being. Melissa Bosch

Introduction

discussed the challenges of being the only Black person in a workplace, and the added difficulty of breaking through the glass ceiling for Black Irish women. The intersectionality of race and gender was highlighted as a barrier to leadership roles within Irish organisations by many of the authors. Winnifred Akinyemi discussed the struggles of Black Irish women as a triple whammy of race, gender, and misrecognition. Emer O'Neill pointed out the disparity in career advancement and pay between male counterparts and the discrimination faced by Black women. Tafadzwa Mandiwanza emphasised the lack of familial and community support for Black women, making it even more challenging to balance work, education, and family responsibilities. Emotional labour featured strongly in the book, where unacknowledged and unpaid extra work, which forms a fundamental pillar of our society is carried out by Black Irish women. The authors stressed the importance of acknowledging the invisible wounds carried by Black Irish women due to discrimination and prejudice. They also highlighted the lack of safe spaces for Black women to address injustices in the workplace. While belonging needs are often advocated for when considering inclusive workplaces, this book and its authors called for acceptance and understanding of Black Irish women to be cultivated in order to create a more inclusive work environment.

Through personal journeys and perspectives shared in this book, we hope to open us up to the experiences, debates, possibilities, and benefits in supporting Black Irish women in Ireland. We recommend a shift in focus from belonging needs in minorities and minoritized groups – because it places the responsibility and deficit in them, and we advocate for a change in language to *'acceptance'* which places the onus of change on the host community and workplace. We also call for equal opportunities for all individuals in the workplace and advocate for positive visibility and representation of Black Irish women. We suggest four key strategies to attaining equity: (i) the practice of equality of experience, (ii) integrating acceptance of difference into all workplace practices, (iii) the provision of safe spaces of interaction and healing, and (iv) a labour market leadership activation and strategic plan for Black Irish women.

Finally, the authors' dedication and openness in sharing their stories have made this project possible, contributing to a broader dialogue on gender equity and inclusion in the workforce. Authors from different sectors, professional background with expertise and insight from diverse Black African descent worked together to create this important book.

References

Crenshaw, K. (1991), 'Mapping the margins: intersectionality, identity politics and violence against women of color', *Stanford Law Review*, 43: 1241–1299.

Economic and Social Research Institute (ESRI) (2023). New ESRI research finds a significant 'migrant wage gap', with East Europeans particularly affected, earning 40% less per hour than Irish counterparts. [online] ESRI. https://www.esri.ie/news/new-esri-research-finds-a-significant-migrant-wage-gap-with-east-europeans-particularly

Joseph, E. (2020). 10 microaggressions in the workplace. Available at: https://roguecollective.ie/ten-microaggressions-in-the-workplace

Joseph, E. (2018), 'Whiteness and racism: examining the racial order in Ireland', *Irish Journal of Sociology*, 26(1): 46–70, doi: 10.1177/0791603517737282.

Joseph, E. (2019), 'Discrimination against credentials in Black bodies: counter-stories of the characteristic labour market experiences of migrants in Ireland', *British Journal of Guidance & Counselling*, 47(4): 524–542, doi: 10.1080/03069885.2019.1620916.

1
Embracing diversity

Ebun Joseph

CEO & founder, Institute of Anti-racism and Black Studies
Coordinator and lecturer Black Studies & Critical Race Theory

1.1 Introduction

From the realm of healthcare to the world of Hollywood, the gender pay gap continues to cast a shadow over the lives of women worldwide. The plight of Black women in the workplace also continues to raise alarming concerns – are they on the verge of vanishing from professional spheres altogether? The tragic loss of Dr Antoinette Candia-Bailey, who took her own life due to relentless bullying, is a poignant reminder of the perils faced by Black women in demanding professions. The recent abrupt resignation of Dr. Claudine Gay, Harvard's only Black female President, amid accusations of plagiarism underscores the pervasive barriers that obstruct the ascent of accomplished Black women, even within institutions of higher learning. In the corridors of the corporate world and academia where the pursuit of knowledge ostensibly reigns supreme, the journey for a Black woman is still full of additional obstacles and barriers.

The challenges for Black women extend well beyond academia, even permeating the glimmering façade of Hollywood. Recently, actresses such as Viola Davis and Taraji P. Henson have boldly confronted their industry's discriminatory practices. Davis's vocal assertions about the stark wage disparities between Black and White actresses, despite equivalent training and talent, resonate as a clarion call for systemic reform. Her impassioned plea for justice echoes the sentiments of countless Black women who have found themselves undervalued and overlooked in the pursuit of their dreams. Henson's admission that she even considered abandoning her craft due to the persistent wage gap is a testament to the toll of systemic inequities.

The struggles faced by Black women are not isolated incidents that happen only in the US; they reflect broader societal disparities that undermine the fundamental principles of equity and fairness. In 2022, 35-year-old NHS doctor, Dr. Vaishnavi Kumar took her own life, leaving a suicide note where, according to her father, she said that people were "belittling her and demeaning her". In Ireland, there are reported cases of dismissals from work without prior warning, long-term mental health issues and stress from mistreatment at work. The pursuit of gender and racial equity is not merely a personal or particular group endeavour – it is a collective struggle that resonates with every ally, activist, and scholar of colour who dares to challenge the status quo. It strikes at the core of society's professed commitment to equity, diversity, and inclusion, and the unbridled pursuit of change, reminding us that until every woman, irrespective of her group is afforded equal opportunities and recognition, the integrity of our society is not intact.

1.2 Authentic acceptance of Black Irish women is missing in many workplaces

The notion of equity prompts a cascade of questions when examining the status of Black Irish women in the labour market. What do we really mean by equity, and who gets to experience it? When we talk about embracing equity, are we directing our conversation to employers, management, and HR professionals who navigate the hiring and firing processes? Or is our dialogue aimed at our colleagues and allies (or those professing to be allies)? Perhaps, we are addressing each other or those intricately woven into the fabric of our lives. What should we aim for, equity or equality, equality of outcomes, or equality of opportunities? Amid our chant of "*no one left behind*," the pursuit of equity is a complex challenge that is not equally experienced by all.

Black employees, both male and female, collectively lack equity in Western society. As well as grappling with race and colour bias, Black women, as a group, usually have to contend with additional issues because of their gender. Black Irish women face a distinct lack of equity within the Irish labour market. Measuring this imbalance proves complicated as it is not just a numbers game. Although gender parity is improving, we know that disparity in labour market outcomes still exist as women continue to be underrepresented in management and senior roles. They earn less than their male counterparts, face poorer working conditions and are prone to bullying and workplace harassment. The book, *Racial Stratification in the Labour Market* (Joseph, 2020) shows how many migrant women are assigned gendered tasks which are on a lower salary scale than their male counterparts. While women in Europe and Ireland have a gender parity of 14.4% –which means women start working for free from 9 November until the end of the year – a recent study in Ireland shows that minority women experience an even greater disparity and have a double penalty when it comes to gender parity. According to the research by the Economic and Social Research Institute (ESRI) and the Department of Children, Equality, Disability, Integration and Youth, the data from 2011 to 2018 showed that 'non-Irish' workers earned 22% less than Irish nationals, or 78 cents for every €1 earned by an Irish worker (2023). 'Non-Irish' workers in Ireland face a significant 'migrant wage gap'. Migrant women, in particular, experienced one of the largest wage gaps and they were reported to face a 'double earnings penalty' for being both female and foreign. It is not about the numbers of Black women present or affected, but about how their qualifications, skills, credentials and their person, which they bring to the world of work are consistently undervalued, and not accepted, leading to their underrepresentation in the professional arena. In essence, the challenge is how Black Irish women are accepted or not accepted in the workplace. This necessitates a comprehensive re-evaluation of systemic biases, a commitment to fair representation, and a collective effort to recognize, appreciate, and empower the credentials, competencies and humanity of Black Irish women in the labour force.

1.3   Who experiences equity?

A core issue lies in the devaluation of qualifications attributed to Black Irish women. Despite possessing comparable skills and expertise, their contributions are frequently overlooked, leading to a systemic undervaluing of their potential. This devaluation contributes to their underrepresentation in the workforce, exacerbating the struggle for equity. Interestingly, this also happens to competencies even when they relate to skills and contributions obtained in Ireland (Joseph, 2019; 2022). The intersectionality of race and gender further compounds the challenges. Black and African Irish women grapple with unique hurdles that stem from the interconnected aspects of their identity as Black women and not from not their race alone (i.e., being Black) or gender (i.e., being female). The combination of race and gender forms a new identity as Black Irish women. There is a lack of acceptance of Black Irish women which is linked to the colonial past and racist present where Black women are expected to be subservient and have a lower status in their homes, workplace and in the wider society. For example, self-confidence, which is celebrated in other women, is usually perceived negatively in Black women.

Despite the Diversity, Equity and Inclusion (DEI) movement rooted in the 1960s Civil Rights Movement, which has grown to include gender, sexual orientation, religion, country of origin, and other identities, White women occupy 63% of DEI leadership roles (McKinsey et al., 2022). Interestingly, most DEI training and programmes rarely mention race and racism. When intersectionality is mentioned, Black women do not even feature on the list. This is despite the fact that Kimberle Crenshaw developed the concept of intersectionality using Black women's identity and the challenges it creates for them. I focus much of my current work on anti-racism, because in over 20 years of living here, I have encountered, endured, and witnessed many challenges and struggles in the labour market. Will these challenges continue to the younger generations, some of who report as having similar experiences of hardship navigating the labour market except those in areas of skill shortage or specific expertise. Will they have to endure the same struggles as their parents? How can we make the world a better place for them? Many White colleagues and employers in my interactions routinely express the hope that the experiences of this group would be better. Unfortunately, it will not disappear on its own without deliberate action. Racism is like inheriting grandma's house, which might look beautiful on the outside but with 'manky' flooring inside that probably needs to be replaced. There are often items in the house that you may need to get rid of as well. To truly enjoy your inherited house and avoid creaky floorboards, the solution is to get rid of that manky floor and put in new flooring. It will involve making some structural changes. Racism is like this house with the manky floors. We have inherited a space [racist] that is unhealthy for everyone. We all have the responsibility to either continue to live in the house that way or make the change. Racism operates on two key principles, power and policy. Real change must be systemic. It must change the policy/policies and laws that have institutionalised that particular racism. Most people want to hear about the study of culture and cultural differences or the 3-D approach, Dance, Dining and Dress (Srivastava, 2007)—this cannot change racism.

1.4 The cost of equity to the Black Irish woman

Reflecting on my 22 years in Ireland, I must acknowledge the challenges I've faced as a Black Irish woman. While I may have progressed in my career, I faced an uphill battle from the beginning. With a background in microbiology, I made a career shift upon arriving in Ireland, becoming an IACP certified counsellor in 2007, and a Career Guidance Consultant in 2009 after completing a postgraduate diploma and master's degree in 2010. I went on to study for a PhD in social justice (Equality Studies) from 2012 to 2016. What struck me at that time was the disparity in opportunities for individuals from different backgrounds. While working in an organisation that supported migrants entering the Irish job market, it was disheartening to see that our Black clients often spent up to 2 years seeking unpaid work, while their Western European counterparts usually secured paid employment in a 2–6-month period. Although our Eastern European clients faced language barriers, they usually found employment within a year with the right support from our programme. Clients of Black African descent, however, faced a frustrating cycle of being told they lacked experience or qualifications, leading them to continually retrain and volunteer in the hope of securing a job. Despite their efforts, many found themselves stuck in a cycle of rejection (Joseph, 2018; 2022). In some cases, volunteers were even asked to onboard new staff for the same jobs they had not been recruited for! The cost of equity is not just measured in terms of the time and effort it takes to navigate a biased system, but in the emotional toll of constantly being overlooked and undervalued. Having to be four times better to attain a role leaves many people of colour feeling frustrated, knowing that they are overqualified and underemployed. Despite these challenges, Black Irish women are continuing to push forward, in the hope that they will eventually be recognized and get the opportunities they deserve.

1.5 A counter story of a young Black Irish woman's job termination experience

In 2023, I received a phone call from a young woman called Kemi (not her real name) who was seeking support after a troubling experience at her workplace. It's not uncommon for me to receive distressing calls from individuals facing workplace discrimination, as many now see me as a trusted source of help for people who have been negatively impacted. Despite claims from racism monitoring systems that incidents are not being reported, I continue to hear first-hand accounts from those who have been impacted by racism. The issue lies not with individuals being unwilling to report, but with the systems in place for collecting and addressing these reports. It is like asking a female rape victim to report her assault to a room full of men – this would never be done; neither is it effective. The reality is that victims of racism often find themselves in a system where those in positions of power and authority are predominantly White, making it difficult for them to come forward. Why do we do it when it's racism? Victims of racism are often in situation where the EDI manager is White, the CEO to escalate the report to is White, the manager implicated in performing the discrimination/racism is White, the court to report to is all White, the recommended mediator from the redress board is White and the independent reporting system is monitored by White people. In order to truly address issues of racism in the workplace, we must examine and challenge the existing structures that perpetuate inequality. It is through listening to, and amplifying the voices of, those affected by racism that we can begin to create meaningful change.

In this section, I have developed a counter story based on real reports, to shed light on the challenges faced by individuals seeking justice and support in the face of workplace discrimination.

Story A: Stock story between a Black Irish woman fired from her role after only one month in the job and her line manager

The setting

Kemi, a 26-year-old Black Irish woman living in Dublin, has just begun a job at a service company. She is the only Black person in the organisation, as the only other Black person left before she started working there. She was called into her line manager's office and told that she was being let go from the job because she did not meet her target for the first month.

Story A: Kemi's story

[Phone rings]

Line Manager: Hello, Kemi, please can you come to my office?

Kemi: Okay. I will be with you in a minute.

Line Manager: I am sorry to tell you this, but we have to let you go. You have not met your target and this is important to us.

Kemi: [*heart starts to thump loudly*] I am sure I can improve once I get more familiar with the tasks. There are also other staff here who are not meeting their target. I have only been here one month.

Line manager: You don't have to worry or talk about other people. This is about you, you are not making your target and we have to let you go.

Kemi: Oh. When does this take effect?

Line Manager: Immediately.

Kemi: I have things I am working on. I can complete it and others can take over the case.

Line Manager: You don't need to work off any hours, you have to leave now.

Kemi [*heart thumping, uncertain if she should protest, then decides otherwise*] Okay. That's fine. [*She walks out of the manager's office in the direction of her office.*]

Kemi: [*She arrives back in the shared office and said to her colleagues*] Guys! I have just been let go!

Line Manager: [*She appeared at the door of Kemi's office which she shared with other colleagues.* You have to clear your desk and hand over your IT system and badge. [*She stood there and watched Kemi until she cleared her desk, closed down the computer and left the office*].

***

Story B: Counter story between young Black Irish women recently fired from her role and a Black anti-racism activist

Kemi: Thank you Dr. Uzo for taking the time to meet me.

Dr. Uzo: It's fine. I wish I was meeting you under better circumstances. What happened? How do you get fired within a month of starting a new job? For anyone to legally fire a member of staff, there are steps that must be taken which would take time and longer than the 1 month you had in the role. Tell me what happened.

Kemi: I started this job and I was the only Black person there. I was later told that there was one other Black person before but that they left. I was not told the circumstances surrounding their departure.

Dr. Uzo: I was going to ask if there are other Black staff there. Okay.

Kemi: The line manager seemed nice enough when I first started. I actually thought I was doing well. I was making an effort with the team, I was relating and collaborating on issues when needed. My figures were not bad as well. The number of cases I was processing per allotted time was reasonable. So, you can see my surprise, when the line manager called me and told me I was being terminated with immediate effect. My heart almost dropped out of my body but I could not say much.

Dr. Uzo: Did you get two warnings that your targets were low and you would have to work faster? Did your manager put any plan in place to support you on how you could reach your target? Did she ask a senior colleague who meets their target to speak to you and give you any help?

Kemi: No, there was no plan or support and no prior issue was ever raised about my speed. I was just told I did not meet the target and I was to stop working immediately.

Dr. Uzo: That cannot be legal. You have to have some form of warning, and intervention to support you if a problem was identified.

Kemi: The thing that upset me the most was that the line manager came and stood over me, watching me pack up my things and go. Dr. Uzo...I felt like a criminal...They had a Black staff member before me. That person is gone as well. Maybe she just uses that role to service the 'need' to have a person of colour but she doesn't really want us there. She was very quick to let me go. It has been so hard for me since then. I keep thinking maybe it is me who is not capable. It has made me start to doubt myself when I know I am very capable.

***

Kemi's story is not an isolated incident. It sheds light on the lack of support, due process, and isolation experienced by those facing discrimination and racism. Despite promises that racism would improve for the next generation, Kemi, a 26-year-old young woman in Ireland faced the challenge of being fired from her job without the usual rigour required to decide if a staff member can carry out a job or not. The lack of support for victims of discrimination in Ireland leaves many afraid to speak up, for the fear of repercussions in a close-knit community where everyone knows each other. Why do people get away with it? It's because there is not enough support. In Ireland, the onus is on the victim to prove the discrimination. This is just one example, I receive so many reports from young people who have been fired from their jobs, or face disciplinary procedures, or aggression when they report racism or the senior management turns it around and accuses the staff member of being incompetent in their roles. Reports have come from international students, healthcare staff, professionals being infantilised in management roles. The list is endless.

1.6. Equity can only be achieved by deliberate action

Securing gender equity is a pressing issue as we often overlook the intersecting identities of Black Irish women. Black Irish women are not just defined by their gender, but also by their race. For instance, the experiences of a Black woman are vastly different from those of a White woman, as race is not a factor for the latter.

Similarly, a Traveller woman, although White, faces discrimination due to her ethnicity, highlighting the complexities of intersectionality. In order to achieve equity for Black Irish women, a comprehensive and deliberate approach is needed. This involves shifting the narrative to value the qualifications and contributions of Black women in the workforce, departing from the systemic devaluation of not just their skills but also as a person with equal right to be in these roles. It also requires institutional changes, such as implementing inclusive policies to counter biases in hiring and promotion processes. A gender specific approach in the integration policy is vital.

Education and awareness are also key in addressing the challenges faced by Black Irish women. By understanding the intersectionality of their identities, society can better support and empower Black Irish women. Advocating for legislative changes to address pay disparities and discriminatory practices is essential in promoting economic empowerment for Black Irish women in the labour market. Ultimately, achieving equity for Black Irish women requires a collective effort from individuals, organisations, and society as a whole. It's about actively breaking down systemic barriers, challenging biases, and creating an inclusive environment where Black Irish women can thrive without facing obstacles that have hindered their progress historically. We often talk about belonging needs but I have argued that what we need is acceptance (Joseph, 2020). Embracing equity means taking pro-active steps to advance all groups, including setting quotas and implementing affirmative action to address the unique challenges faced by Black Irish women, particularly in leadership roles, in sectors like academia, funding research, businesses, and groups for/by Black Irish women. If we have set quotas to increase the numbers of women in the workplace, we can do the same for Black Irish women. We require our White sisters to work with us in solidarity – gender applies to all women. Inclusion is not just a concept, it's a commitment to creating a more equitable and supportive society for all.

1.7 Emotional labour of Black and African Irish women

Black Irish women often contribute in ways which go beyond their paid work, highlighting the complex roles they play in society. Through the interviews I conducted for the documentary, it became clear that these women were  deeply involved in community work, caregiving, and in other unpaid roles, all while juggling their professional responsibilities. They also took on many unofficial tasks in the workplace. This dual commitment reflects their sense of responsibility and community engagement, showcasing the invaluable contributions they make in and beyond their jobs. These range from roles in children's schools, to activities in the community, running free classes to fill gaps in services for their community. Sports, boys, men and women's groups all run volunteering. Taking on employee relations group at work to tackle racism and microaggression at work. These extra duties often go unpaid and unacknowledged. They often come under the emotional labour expended by Black people generally, but Black Irish women more specifically. The most egregious is the way many from the Black community who are keen to take on volunteering roles find themselves stuck in a spiral going nowhere, yet they see volunteering working for other groups. I have also had requests where I am expected to give keynote speeches, presentations, anti-racism talks, and advice without compensation. This trend raises questions about societal expectations, gender roles, and the potential for imbalance. It is crucial to re-evaluate these norms and foster an environment that values and recognizes the diverse roles Black Irish women play. By promoting a more equitable distribution of responsibilities and acknowledging the significance of unpaid work, society can help these women to achieve a more balanced integration of their professional and societal contributions, including a balanced work-life.

2
Equity continues to evade Black Irish women in the workplace

Carline Thompson-Kelly
Nurse, Researcher, Author, and Activist

2.1 Introduction

Equity is about everyone receiving the most appropriate access to opportunities in a justified and impartial manner that aids in their overall success (Lead MN, 2018). The founder of the Institute of Anti-racism and Black Studies in Ireland, Dr. Ebun Joseph (*Irish Times*, 2023) reported that the technology and healthcare sectors have a good record in employing people from ethnic groups. Although Black Irish women play an integral role in the Irish labour market, they are far from achieving equity because of 'The Black Ceiling'. Dr. Wendy Oke, the CEO of TeachKloud who coined this phrase explains that the 'Black Ceiling' represents significant barriers that impede progress and opportunities for minority groups, especially Black women in Ireland (Linehan & Sheerin, 2023).

2.2 Why does equity evade Black Irish women?

Black Irish women face pay disparities in comparison to their White Irish counterparts in terms of higher education, qualifications, and promotion prospects (Thompson, 2023). In my experience as a Black Irish woman in the healthcare sector, I always avail of opportunities for continuous professional development. However, my professional development has not received the same recognition or financial compensation from my employer as the equivalent training completed by a White Irish counterpart. Research has shown that non-Irish women experience double-earning disadvantages from being female and a migrant (ESRI, 2023).

Racial discrimination plays a fundamental part in the way Black Irish women navigate the Irish labour market. For example, as a Black Irish woman, I have lived experiences of racial discrimination which included biases, microaggressions, macroaggressions, gaslighting, prejudice, racial profiling, and being overlooked for promotional opportunities and leadership positions. This form of discrimination makes it difficult for women like me to advance in our careers. My recent research on *the experiences of racial discrimination among ethnic minority healthcare professionals in Ireland* (Thompson, 2023), highlighted that minority ethnic healthcare professionals reported receiving racial discrimination from colleagues, families, and patients that negatively impacted their mental health and well-being.

Social exclusion often results in Black women being overlooked, undervalued, left out in decision-making processes as well as work and social outings due to their ethnicity, race, socio-economic, and migration status (Privalko et al., 2023). Social exclusion can sometimes be exacerbated by toxic organisational cultures and can contribute to isolation in the work environment. Equity is enshrined in the concept of social inclusion which emphasises that every individual should reap the benefits of prosperity and enjoy the maximum standard of health and well-being and a safe space to thrive and survive.

Lack of safe spaces and organisational restraint stifles opportunities for equity in the work environment. Minda Harts, in her book *Right Within: How to Heal from Racial Trauma in the Workplace*, showed that a lot of women, especially Black women do not feel safe in their work environment. Their autonomy to advocate for themselves about issues that affect them is often met with negativity and constant gaslighting, making it difficult for them to thrive and survive. For example, a few years ago, after offensive and racial remarks were made towards me at work, I was not allowed to speak up about it. I was compelled to report the person who made the remarks. I was cautioned and formally investigated as the person who made the offensive remarks. This quickly made me realize that there were no safe spaces for me to communicate injustices or seek redress due to intrinsic organizational restraint. During the investigation, I had to contend with discrimination and it was a very traumatic experience and I still had to show up to work throughout the investigation process. There was a huge loss of trust both in my colleagues and managers. Unethical experiences like these contribute to poor labour market outcomes and add to the problems Black women experience in trying to access equity in Ireland.

2.3   Why access to equity is problematic

Accessing equity in Ireland for African Irish women and other minority ethnic groups has been perpetuated by misinformation, misconceptions, and marginalisation by the wider public, and reinforced by governmental and immigration policies (Privalko et al., 2023). Misinformation about minority ethnic groups is often perpetuated by the media and far-right groups who thrive on spreading hate and propaganda. For example, when I first came to Ireland, Black people were viewed as refugees, asylum seekers, uneducated, and social welfare dependents. There is still an ongoing trend and the response to the mention of Black people in Ireland is often a reference to asylum seekers. This is due to a lack of public awareness, education, and training about the integration of immigrants into Irish society. Additionally, skilled and educated migrant workers, including African Irish women who had access to the Irish labour market even though underrepresented were viewed as taking away jobs from their Irish counterparts. Irish immigration policies further compounded these misconceptions. Asylum seekers and refugees who were skilled and educated were not allowed to work until a decision was made on their applications, which for many applicants took years (O'Connell, 2019). Furthermore, immigrants who were recruited for the labour market and had spouses or partners who migrated with them or came to join them at a later date were not allowed access to the labour market, leaving them economically and socially marginalised and disadvantaged (Privalko et al., 2023). Although some of these immigration policies have changed, people from minority ethnic backgrounds still find it difficult to fully integrate into Irish society as equal citizens due to historical barriers.

2.4   Equity in all spaces is possible

Black Irish women *can* have equity in all spaces within Irish society, if action was achieved at policy and organisational levels. Organisations that strive to be diverse, equitable, and inclusive, must intentionally create culturally competent work environments, where Black Irish women are seen, respected, heard, celebrated, and valued as individuals with skills, knowledge, and abilities. They should be seen as people who are ready to participate and not as those who should be infantilised or micromanaged. Any culturally competent work environment should regularly train their staff members about cultural competence and fostering relationships with people from diverse backgrounds to enhance understanding, collaboration and progress in the same way as LGBQTIA+ rights are taught in workplaces.

Policy integration and monitoring is also vital; systematic racism in policies must be eliminated and anti-racism initiatives should be implemented in every area of society. For example, all organisations should adhere and be accountable to the Equal Status Acts 2000–2018 and the Employment Equality Acts 1998–2015 that prohibit discrimination in providing accommodation, goods, services, and education under the nine grounds (Irish Human Rights and Equality Commission, 2020).

Governmental and organisational policies are needed to promote Black women equitably and equally to achieve greater economic stability. Policymakers need to have a deeper understanding of economic realities and the intersectional barriers of Black women and prioritise policy solutions that dismantle barriers. Black Irish women need effective communication, ally-ship and collaboration with their Irish counterparts especially those in leadership positions to break down barriers.

Black women need equal and equitable access to health, education, employment, and pay so they can positively realise their potential in creating better opportunities for themselves and their family and break the cycle of inter-generational poverty.

Organisations should include awareness training on equity, diversity and inclusion. All immigrants should be fully informed about their rights under Irish law as it relates to the Irish labour market. An increase in research and data analysis about Black women's experiences within the labour market and other areas of society is needed to combat current issues and safeguard better solutions now and into the future. Too often, economic policies are adopted without real knowledge of the issues being faced by Black women as a group.

2.5 The workplace is fraught with consequences

It is the norm in many cultures for women to take on the position of homemakers and nurturers, especially those who are mothers. These cultural norms also apply to Black and African Irish women. Nowadays, homemaking and nurturing are considered extra work, especially for women working outside the home to increase their income. As it relates to being employed as a nurse, I must dot all my i's and cross all my t's which is a common cultural phrase, meaning I must finish my assigned work and complete it to the best of my ability. For example, working as a Black Irish woman in the healthcare sector, I cannot walk away from completing my daily assigned duties without facing the consequences of my actions. However, some of my White Irish counterparts can walk away from their assigned duties without being reprimanded. This can sometimes place a burden on us Black women to complete our duties and the duties of our White Irish counterparts, leading to burnout.

Thompson (2023) confirmed that most of the workload was either left for minority ethnic healthcare professionals to complete or was delegated to them by their White colleagues/managers. This research further highlighted that minority ethnic healthcare professionals were willing to take on extra paid work of their choosing to boost their weekly/monthly income capacity. In fact, it is not uncommon to see professional Black and African Irish women running small businesses, volunteering in their communities, and networking to enhance their earning potential. This was true for me in 2023 when I decided, after years of procrastination, to launch a baking and pastry business to give the Irish public a taste of Jamaican products with an Irish twist. Women are often seen as the pillars of society and take on dominant positions and roles in the household and their work environments. Hence, I believe that both paid and unpaid work that contributes to the welfare of the individual and their family should be equally recognized. I also believe that when Black African Irish women are recognized for contributing to society, they will excel in their daily lives, careers, and work environments. In many cases, companies don't realise that not giving Black and African Irish women their due recognition within the workplace will be detrimental in the future.

2.6 Find out why Carline Thompson's day is from 5 a.m. to midnight!

I came to Ireland in 2003 on a work permit under the work and study programme. I went from Dublin to Tipperary to Cork and back to Dublin to secure employment, all of which took almost a year. During the process of employment, my employer declined to take on the financial responsibility of renewing my work permit. I decided to extend my visa by entering further education. While working as a pastry chef, I graduated with a certificate in Technology and Business Studies in 2006 from Grafton College of Management. In 2006 I began a bachelor's degree in intellectual disabilities nursing at Trinity College, Dublin. While attending Trinity College, my days started at 5 a.m. and ended at midnight. As I had to commute to college and get there before 9 a.m. with a 15-minute grace period. College finished at 5 p.m. and I then had to go to work as a healthcare assistant from 6 p.m. until 10 p.m. If I was late to work, I had to make up the time. When I arrived home at midnight, I sometimes had to catch up on my college assignments. In 2010, I completed my degree in nursing and I started working as an intellectual disability nurse. I also resumed my studies at Trinity College where I pursued a master's degree in disability studies and in 2012, I graduated with a master's degree with honours. Navigating college and work was difficult but I was resilient and committed. In 2013, my son joined me in Ireland and I now had to navigate working and raising him. As a nurse and single mother, I had to balance my work, my family, and educating myself and my son. I faced tremendous inequalities in my job but had to keep going as I was the breadwinner in my household. My master's degree in disability studies and experience did not lead to any promotions and I usually worked for managers who were less qualified than me. This experience further propelled me to pursue another master's degree in healthcare management and I graduated in 2023 with a master's degree with distinction.

I have shared the ideas I have learned through research from both master's degrees in conferences and networking events in Abu Dhabi, Dubai, Hawaii, Ireland, Northern Ireland and Saudi Arabi to promote awareness and hopefully widen opportunities for other minorities to follow. I recently presented my research about the experiences of racial discrimination among ethnic minority healthcare professionals in Ireland at the 16th European Public Health Association Conference held in Dublin, and it was warmly received. Audience members showed interest in learning more about the minority ethnic community as it relates to racial discrimination. In December 2022, Sister's Heart Consult Ireland, a minority community organisation, awarded me the title of Queen for 2023 to represent them at selected events and charity activities as an honorary ambassador and mentor. In 2023, I co-wrote with

Susuana Komolafe *Building Our Network*. In November 2023, I launched my pastry business and have travelled around the country introducing a taste of Jamaica through the many flavours of banana bread I produce.

I am still working to build my business's reach internationally. I am also still working as a nurse in the intellectual disability community in Dublin. I hope to use the skills and experiences gained to further my career in healthcare management and education. After 14 years in a career as a nurse, "still I rise". I rise because I know that I am doing God's work. I rise because I know that my journey as a healthcare professional is a pivotal part of my destiny as a Black Irish woman, and I am thankful. I rise because I know better days are ahead, no matter the circumstances. I am now an author, small business owner, nurse researcher, and anti-racism activist. I have a bachelor's degree and two master's degrees from one of the most prestigious colleges in the Western Hemisphere. I am humbled and I am proud of where I am, and what I have achieved. I will continue to rise and excel. I encourage every Black Irish woman in the words of the late Bob Marley to "…Get up, stand up, stand up for your right, get up, stand up, don't give up the fight…"

References

Economic and Social Research Institute (2023). *New ESRI research finds a significant 'migrant wage gap', with East Europeans particularly affected, earning 40% less per hour than Irish counterparts*. [online] ESRI.
https://www.esri.ie/news/new-esri-research-finds-a-significant-migrant-wage-gap-with-east-europeans-particularly

Harts, M. (2021). *Right Within*. Seal Press.

Irish Human Rights and Equality Commission (2020). *THE EQUAL STATUS ACTS 2000–2018*. [online]
https://www.ihrec.ie/app/uploads/2022/08/IHREC-Equal-Status-Rights-Leaflet-WEB.pdf

Lead M.N (2018). *What is equity and what do we mean by it? | Lead MN*. [online] www.leadmn.org. Available at: https://www.leadmn.org/EDI-series1

Linehan, P.M. and Sheerin, D.C. (2023). The Black Ceiling: Employment Experiences of Women of Colour in Southwest Ireland. *Dept. of Organisation & Professional Development Publications*. [online] https://doi.org/10.34719/VUZY6228

O'Connell, P.J. (2019). Why are so few Africans at work in Ireland? Immigration policy and labour market disadvantage. *Irish Journal of Sociology*, p.079160351985376. https://doi.org/10.1177/0791603519853767

Olatunji Komolafe, S. and Thompson-Kelly, C. (2023). Building our Network. SOM PR Consultancy.

Privalko, I., McGinnity, F., Curristan, S. and Enright, S. (2023). How Do Migrants Fare in the Irish Labour Market? Country of Origin, Gender, Asylum and Ethnicity Effects. *Journal of Immigrant & Refugee Studies*, pp.1–18. https://doi.org/10.1080/15562948.2023.2196664

The Irish Times (2023). *Is there racial equality in the Irish workforce? Up to a point...* [online] The Irish Times. https://www.irishtimes.com/special-reports/2023/10/13/is-there-racial-equality-in-the-irish-workforce-up-to-a-point/

Thompson, C. (2023). The experience of racial discrimination among ethnic minority healthcare professionals in Ireland. *European journal of public health*, [online] 33(Supplement_2). https://doi.org/10.1093/eurpub/ckad160.059

3

Barriers to gaining equity for Black Irish women

Melissa Bosch,
Head of Diversity, Equity, and Inclusion, EY Ireland

3.1 Introduction

Ireland has changed demographically over the past two decades. This has been marked by a significant rise in ethnic diversity that has welcomed a kaleidoscope of cultures, colours, perspectives, and experiences. Not only have I witnessed this change, but I have also contributed to it. What I have observed is that women, who embody the intersection of Black, Irish, and female identities, face a layered bias that is often overlooked. They form an integral piece of our society but are often relegated to the sidelines. This diverse medley should ideally shine in the inclusive spirit of humanity. Unfortunately, like many places globally, Ireland struggles with equitable representation within its labour market. For many Black Irish women, attaining true equity is still a significant challenge. Although Ireland prides itself on being a diverse society, recent studies reveal there is significant work to be done to bolster diversity, equity, and inclusion in the workforce. According to a survey carried out by the Irish Human Rights and Equality Commission in 2020, over half of the Black respondents reported experiencing some form of racial discrimination, and 42% said they had been discriminated against due to their race when in work or when applying for work. So, while Ireland has made substantial strides in promoting diversity and inclusivity, there will never be an equitable labour market until the barriers faced by Black Irish women who work there are recognized and addressed.

3.2 Layered prejudice

Owing to the interconnected biases of race and gender, Black Irish women face a double disadvantage, often dealing with both racial discrimination and gender bias. These obstacles can manifest in various forms, including restricted access to quality job opportunities, lower wages compared to their White counterparts, persistent stereotypes, and reduced career advancement prospects. Moreover, the glass ceiling that prevents women from reaching high-ranking positions in the workplace is even further away for Black women. The intersectionality of race and gender compounds these barriers, so it is no surprise that Black women's representation in leadership roles within Irish organisations is extremely low.

3.3 Embedding equity

Our goal should not only be about equal opportunities; we need to strive for equity - a system that recognizes unequal starting places (Joseph, 2020) and makes provisions for everyone to have access to the same opportunities. For this, we must first acknowledge that not all wounds are visible, that many Black Irish Women carry scars etched deep within their psyche, inflicted by discrimination, prejudice, and stereotyping. Ireland has taken significant steps towards enhancing diversity and inclusion through laws and regulations such as the Employment Equality Acts and the Equality Act. Organisations are beginning to understand the value of a diverse workforce and are actively incorporating diversity and inclusion strategies into their business models.

But we need to do more by imagining a working world where diversity is not simply tolerated but celebrated, where every unique voice contributes to the symphony of human experience. We should pride ourselves on our differences as much as on our shared humanity. So that when we think about equity, it is not merely a slogan to us but a clear call to action. Equity is more than equality, where everyone gets the same. Instead, it sets forth the duty to ensure that everyone gets what they actually need. This means understanding the nuanced struggles faced by marginalised minority groups in our society like Black Irish women. We must bridge the gap, not by creating 'one-size-fits-all' solutions, but by tailoring them to address the unique experiences of Black Irish women.

3.4 Inaccessibility of equal opportunities for all groups

Much of my work is about influencing and advocating for an environment where everyone feels valued, respected, and heard. Yet, we continue to grapple with the problem of equity, especially for Black Irish women, who face the barriers of racial, ethnic, and gender bias. The challenge for Black Irish women, as it is for any minority population, is access to equal opportunities -

for hiring, promotion, or professional development. Black Irish women further encounter issues such as inequities in accessing professional networks, limited representation in leadership roles, and the wage gap. This inequity is often reinforced by networks of privilege that sustain and endorse the existing power structure within organisations.

3.4.1 Battling bias, stereotyping, and microaggressions

Unlike open discrimination, biases operate by subtly influencing decisions related to hiring, promotion, and allocation of opportunities. Biases are often deep-rooted and subconscious. They permeate the workspace, intertwining within the threads of the organisational culture, in the way people communicate, behave, and make decisions. To address these hidden biases, organisations need systematic policies and practices aimed at fostering cultural competence, self-awareness, and reducing the influence of stereotypes on critical decision-making processes. Stereotyping, albeit mostly unconscious, might limit the opportunities available to minority groups and restrict their upward mobility in the organisation.

Microaggressions are a prevalent issue for minority groups in workplaces. "Your English is so good. You're so eloquent!" might seem like a compliment but it carries the underlying assumption that racial minority individuals cannot speak fluent English, reinforcing stereotypes and subtly suggesting that they are seen as foreigners in their own country. Subtle and seemingly minor, these incidents carry a significant and enduring impact on the person's confidence, morale, and productivity (see Joseph, 2020 for her article on 10 microaggressions in the workplace). Leaders must candidly address and call out such harmful incidents, and foster a culture of openness and understanding.

3.4.2 A token Black woman

By the same token, no one wants to be appointed into a position because of a diversity policy. Tokenism is as a glaring issue, reducing Black women's roles to mere representative figures for affirmative action. This superficiality undervalues their true merit, and reinforces discriminatory perceptions rather than dismantling them. Tokenism casts a long, othering shadow, isolating Black women and alienating them in their professional environment. No one wants to be seen by one aspect of their identity. However, the intrinsic privilege afforded to one group over another needs to be bravely and authentically addressed within organisations to ensure equal opportunities for advancement.

3.4.3 Overqualification and underutilisation

It is quite common for Black Irish women, (as is the case for a significant portion of the migrant population), to be working in roles where they are overqualified. The deeply ingrained systemic biases and a lack of opportunity limits talented Black Irish women to positions for which they are overeducated and underutilised. A survey undertaken by the Economic and Social Research Institute (ESRI) in 2020 showed that non-EU migrants had the highest rates of overqualification, indicating a common pattern among minorities of working in roles for which they were overqualified. Black Irish women, as part of this demographic, shared in this experience, often finding themselves stagnating in job roles that do not optimally utilise their skills or qualifications (Joseph, 2020).

3.4.4 Underrepresentation

Black Irish women, like many others from diverse backgrounds, often suffer from the syndrome of often being the only Black woman in the room, or even in the company. This lack of representation in the workforce, and especially in leadership roles, deprives them of role models and amplifies their feelings of isolation. Organisation leaders need to break this cycle because representation at all levels, especially leadership, is essential. Not only would this break the stereotyping and unconscious bias that often closes doors to Black Irish women, but it would also offer role models and mentors who can help foster an environment of inclusion and acceptance.

3.4.5 What's worse than the fear of getting it wrong?

Discussing the lived experience of Black Irish women in the workplace can often be uncomfortable for people from the dominant culture, race, and/or gender. This discomfort may stem from fear of offending someone, of stepping on cultural nuances they don't understand, or exposing their lack of knowledge about the unique challenges Black Irish women may face. This avoidance (which can look like denial to allies and victims) can inadvertently perpetuate systemic racism and unconscious bias in the workplace. It can also stifle critical conversations, making it difficult for organisations to address and combat racial disparities effectively. Furthermore, it can lead to a feeling of isolation for

Black Irish women employees, who might feel that their experiences are being overlooked or ignored. It is crucial to create a safe and supportive environment to discuss these topics openly and honestly, encouraging understanding, and fostering inclusion.

3.5 What do we need for Black women to have equity?

The journey towards equity for Black Irish women begins with acknowledging the intersections of their identity which results in dual discrimination. If the unique challenges that this presents to Black women is not acknowledged and understood, then how can true equity be achieved for them?

3.5.1 Go beyond the rhetoric

Creating a genuinely inclusive culture within an organisation is about making everyone feel not only included, and that they belong and are valued as part of the team. This means it is essential to build a culture where open dialogue about race and gender issues is encouraged and can be openly discussed without fear. Facilitated discussion forums, awareness sessions, and workshops can help foster understanding and empathy among employees, thereby contributing to an increasingly inclusive atmosphere.

Monitoring and tracking progress on diversity and equity initiatives against benchmarks and measurable objectives to ensure accountability is essential. This will generate data-driven insights that can support the development of equity-focussed policies and guidelines. From fair hiring practices to equal pay, policy changes can play a useful role in shaping an equitable environment.

Constraints around collecting sensitive data and a lack of qualitative data on the experiences of Black Irish women in the labour market and workplace has created a barrier for meaningful, data-led conversations in the workplace. However, data constraints should not be used as an excuse to suppress an exploration of the existing broader data sets and individual narrative evidence which collectively show a continued struggle against discrimination and bias.

3.5.2 Stop defaulting to the comfort zone

This is, I believe, a fundamental challenge. Individuals need to challenge their fear of discussing the topic of race and ethnicity, suspend their beliefs, preferences, and traditions, and commit to educating themselves about different lived experiences. It is too easy to default to stereotyping and an attitude of 'Ah sure we are all the same'. This will not foster a culture of belonging. The understanding that Black Irish women face discrimination not just based on their gender, but also on their race and cultural background, is fundamental. 'I don't see colour' only serves the person saying it, as it absolves them of seeing the world from someone else's perspective.

Aggrieved entitlement is another defence mechanism, where historically privileged groups such as White males feel wronged when equal opportunities are extended to marginalised individuals. This behaviour fuels damaging narratives and reflects a sense of unjust loss due to societal shifts towards diversity, equity, and inclusion. When paired with assumptions about minority readiness, commercial impact, or attrition issues, it exacerbates exclusion in the workforce.

Challenging the status quo requires people to lean into the discomfort. It requires the vulnerability, openness, and commitment of both parties: those in positions of privilege, to recognize their power and build emotional and cultural intelligence, and minority groups to raise their voices and share their lived experience to clearly call it out when othering occurs.

3.5.3 Support access to targeted development programmes

Creating equity for Black women in the professional space necessitates fostering robust networks and enhancing their social capital. This can be achieved through mentorship, sponsorship, career coaching, and reverse mentorship. Traditional mentorship and sponsorship offer Black Irish women advice, advocacy, and guidance from seasoned professionals, which can be invaluable in navigating career progression. A career coach can provide targeted strategies for personal growth and skill development. Meanwhile, reverse mentorship, where Black Irish women mentor individuals in senior positions, provides dual benefits. It serves as a platform for Black women to demonstrate their competencies, leadership, and unique perspectives. Also, it enlightens mentors about the realities of systemic racial bias, helping them become powerful allies in promoting inclusivity. Together, these strategies consolidate professional networks, develop social capital, and play an essential role in achieving true workplace equity.

While progress has been made towards diversity and inclusion for minority groups in Ireland, true equity for Black Irish women is a substantial undertaking. This challenge calls for commitment and introspection, benefiting not only Black Irish women, but also organisations and society at large. Overcoming this requires leaders to foster an environment that allows each member, regardless of identity, to reach their potential and contribute to a diverse, innovative workforce. It is necessary to sow seeds of acceptance and nurture understanding, echoing calls for justice. Beyond mere inclusion, striving for belonging, where everyone, especially our intersectional demographic of Black Irish women, feel safe and heard in decision-making is the goal.

3.6 Most Black Irish women are using emotional labour

Women, including those of African/Black heritage living in Ireland, continue to shoulder a disproportionate amount of unpaid work (e.g., housework, caregiving, or volunteering) compared to their male counterparts, in additional to holding down jobs. Socio-cultural norms in Western and African society place value on women's propensity to be caregivers, and the expectation is that it is the woman's job to do everything from care for children, to manage finances, to remember everyone's birthday, to keep the kitchen stocked.

As a diversity, equity, and inclusion (DE&I) leader, I have observed that this 'extra work' (and the associated mental load that women carry) is often unacknowledged and unpaid, and yet forms a fundamental pillar of our society. The roots of this discrepancy lie in deep-seated, societal expectations and gender roles.

3.6.1 Invisible emotional labour

Women in marginalised communities often engage in catch-up work, in an effort to compensate for systemic disadvantages and to make extra income. To level the playing field and build affinity with the majority population, they feel that they should build networks and connections cross culturally, while editing or being hyper-aware of aspects of their ethnicity that they may need to 'tone down' to 'fit in' to make those in positions of power and privilege comfortable to welcome them in. Yet another subtle, but persistent obstacle is a Black woman's 'tone'. Her passion is misconstrued as aggression and her assertiveness is termed as combativeness. Consequently, many women must face the exhausting ordeal of modulation, or muting or toning down their voices to meet pre-defined 'acceptable' norms.

The lack of representation of Black women in professional environments is a contributing factor. This lack of representation can lead to them taking on the unpaid extra work of fighting for diversity, advocating for change, and mentoring other Black women. Many Black Irish women carry the unspoken burden of invisible emotional labour. The societal expectation to stand strong against adversity often leaves them no space to express their genuine feelings, compounding stress, and contributing to depleting mental health.

3.6.2 Battling tokenism

Deep-seated racial and gender biases continue to pervade our workplaces, erecting significant barriers that specifically impede the professional journeys of Black Irish women. Despite making essential contributions to the labour market, Black Irish women find themselves embattled with systemic obstacles ranging from tokenism to mental health impacts that undermine their potential.

Reflecting on my own journey, I, too, have experienced the impact and strain of this 'extra work'. Despite my position as a DE&I Lead, I, too, am not immune to the social and professional pressures faced by Black Irish women. Battling bias, advocating for diversity and fairness, and juggling multiple roles at work, and in my community while intentionally working on my cultural integration, without diluting myself. These extra responsibilities form an unspoken part of my day-to-day life.

In the quest for true diversity, equity, inclusion, and belonging, we must acknowledge and address the unseen labour often performed by Black Irish women. Unpaid 'extra work' is a critical DE&I issue – one that is emblematic of broader systemic inequities. By valuing and supporting the entire spectrum of women's work, we can make strides towards achieving true gender and ethnic equity.

3.7 Meet Melissa Bosch –'Meeting Nelson Mandela was a catalyst for my life's work'

My journey as a female ethnic minority role model is enriched with unique experiences that have assisted my progress to Head of Diversity, Equity, and Inclusion at EY. Raised in South Africa during and after apartheid, I saw at first hand the pervasive societal inequities which sparked my resolve to champion for social justice.

A seminal moment was meeting Nelson

Mandela when I was a teenager. It was a life-changing encounter that gave me a unique perspective on social justice. I remember his towering yet gentle presence, his soft-spoken determination, and the spark in his clouded eyes that spoke of unyielding resilience. His unrelenting commitment to social justice and his magnanimous spirit in the face of adversity inspired me. He personified the essence of sacrifice for a cause greater than oneself. When we met, he held my hand and told me that I was a brave young lady. That moment reminds me that social justice is not a passive belief but a dynamic mission that demands unequivocal resolve, resilience, and courage. It etched in me a deeper sense of responsibility and determination. I didn't know it at the time but it was the catalyst for my life's work.

Throughout my career I observed a disconnection between organisational and societal rhetoric, and representative inclusive practices. It stirred my desire for transformative change. The evident lack of representation and unequal distribution of power provided further motivation.

After moving to Ireland, I focussed on aligning my professional career to my values which are seeded in the African philosophy of 'Ubuntu' which emphasises community, reciprocity, and interdependence. With this strong belief in the universal bond of sharing that connects all humanity, I intentionally grew my network leveraging my experiences, and transferable skills from various professional roles, board appointments, and charitable work. I then galvanised my experience with ongoing learning and mentoring to change career from Marketing and Communications to Diversity, Equity, and Inclusion (DE&I). During my career in DE&I, I have designed and delivered strategies and diversity initiatives, implemented programmes for marginalised groups, and trained employees to embed DE&I practices in the workplace. Challenges along the way only fuelled my determination, and I studied for a master's degree in DE&I, which accredited my experiences and expanded my professional network. I continue to be committed to learning because DE&I is constantly evolving and I continue to advocate for the benefits of diversity in stimulating innovation, increasing employee satisfaction, and profitability.

I consider Ireland to be my home now, I identify as Afro-Irish and I am happy to be contributing to the ever-evolving diversity of the country. So, beyond my professional role, I leverage my skills to promote board diversity, empower executive teams on equitable decision making, and contribute to high-impact community initiatives. Reflecting on my journey, I believe my strength lies in effecting and influencing people-centric change by putting humanity at the heart of design. I believe the power lies not just in attaining my position, but in influencing change using my unique perspective.

Nelson Mandela's words were indeed prophetic. I <u>am</u> a brave young lady. I have courageously presented an authentic perspective on equity, inclusion, and belonging, one that extends beyond words into action. My heritage reminds me that change comes through patience, perseverance, and grit. And that through the power of the collective, we can achieve social justice, equity, inclusion, and belonging for all.

References

Economic and Social Research Institute (2023). New ESRI research finds a significant 'migrant wage gap', with East Europeans particularly affected, earning 40% less per hour than Irish counterparts. [online] ESRI.

https://www.esri.ie/news/new-esri-research-finds-a-significant-migrant-wage-gap-with-east-europeans-particularly

Joseph, E. (2020). 10 microaggressions in the workplace. Available at: https://roguecollective.ie/ten-microaggressions-in-the-workplace

4

Unconscious bias affects equity for Black Irish women in the labour market

Emer O'Neill
Teacher, author, broadcaster and public speaker

4.1 Introduction

Many Black Irish women have not experienced equity in the Irish labour market. My experiences with inequity and employment were driven by other people's lack of understanding of culture, of difference and of the positive influence cultural diversity has in the workplace. Peoples' unconscious bias plays a crucial role in why Black Irish women do not have as many opportunities or equal access to the labour force. Historically, people of African descent have been portrayed as less educated, trustworthy, and professional than their counterparts. These archaic stereotypes are still very real in the 21st century, in Ireland and across the globe. The common experience of the Black Irish community is that we are never quite 'enough'. Being told that we need more experience and more education to advance in our careers, while at the same time watching our peers and colleagues move forward in theirs with similar or less experience or education.

It is not hard to see the proof of this when the lack of ethnic diversity in government, state jobs, the media, NGOs and across positions of leadership is so striking. A quick visit to official websites for the positions in any Irish organisation and click 'Meet our team' or 'Our staff' will provide you with the stark evidence. We are seeing many people from the Black Irish community become the first in many spaces in the labour force in Ireland. Not because there has not been a population of educated and capable people there to conquer these 'firsts' or be present in these spaces, but because of how difficult it has been to access these opportunities. Connection to relevant "networks" or what we often term – who you know and where you come from – can at times hold more weight than any qualifications or experience. Women coming from ethnic minority communities are automatically at a disadvantage due to this. Many Black Irish women have the highest rates of unemployment in the country, while at the same time being the highest educated people per capita in Ireland. Let us take a minute to let that sink in and ask ourselves why.

4.2 Navigating hurdles in the workplace

Unconscious bias and a lack of cultural understanding are at the heart of the inequity Black Irish women face. The lack of accountability, policies, laws, and protection are among the reasons it continues. In 2014 I returned to Ireland after 10 years spent studying and working in the United States. I returned as a qualified teacher with a master's degree in education and 5 years of teaching experience. Despite this, it took me 3 years to secure a teaching position. I received interviews for 80% of the jobs I applied for, so my qualifications and experience were appropriate for the jobs I was applying for, but being successful at the interview stage took such a long time. Obviously, I suspected that "maybe *I (or my colour and ethnicity)*" was really the issue but of course I was unable to fully document or prove this. However, what is clear is that I was a woman of colour trying to access a predominantly White occupation. This predicament is not something new for members of minority groups to experience. We as women have for centuries had to fight against discrimination in the labour force, trying to navigate our way in workplaces traditionally dominated by men; trying to prove that we are good enough and that we belong in these spaces and finding it difficult to prove the discrimination that exists. With the introduction of gender equality policy and strategy, we have seen some changes in pay and opportunity for Irish women, but the struggles of Black Irish women in the workplace still remain with little or no policy or strategy for future change.

I have seen similar stories surrounding accessibility to the labour force for women in the Black Irish community in my activist work. So much so that the alignment of experiences is hard to ignore. When we do not have research studies or data on an issue like this, we must rely on people's lived experiences for information. When a common pattern emerges between the lived experiences of Black Irish women who don't know each other there may well be underlying issue that need further examination. Many Black Irish women have reported having a lot of difficulty in securing an interview for many positions they applied for. A friend of mine spent months applying to jobs after becoming newly qualified. After becoming disheartened with the lack of interview opportunities she was receiving she wondered if her Kenyan name on her CV might be hindering her attempts so she changed the surname on her CV to her White Irish married name and re-applied to the jobs. As quickly as her CVs were sent, she starting receiving interview invitations from the same companies that had ignored or rejected her application only weeks before. This indicates that many of the companies she was applying to saw the name on her CV as a deterrent. The inequality and discrimination out there may shock many but incidents like this are commonplace. Simply having a unique 'non-traditional' name can be enough for an employer not to pursue a candidate, despite their qualifications. Some more forward-thinking organisations use blind screening when screening CVs. Blind screening is a method used to eliminate unconscious bias by removing unnecessary information such as gender, age, racial background, and name. By doing this, it reduces unconscious bias effect in the CV screening process and it helps the most qualified people to be given a chance to interview for the jobs.

Potential employers usually assume from my name that I am a White Irish woman, resulting in some uncomfortable encounters at interview. One such memorable experience was the looks of confusion on the interview panel member's faces when I entered the interview room for a teaching job. This was not the "Emer O'Neill" they expected to see. Before I had a chance to even introduce myself, one of the interviewers blurted out that "the planned part of the interview in Irish would be skipped" – in other words, my brown skin meant I did not speak our native language. There was no malice in the statement, I think they thought the situation was comical. Not only did I not look like an Emer O'Neill but I had been invited to interview for a position that was meant for someone who speaks Irish!

Ironically, I love the Irish language, I can speak it 'cuibheasach' maith' (relatively well) and both of my children attend 'gaelscoileanna' (Irish language-medium schools). I am Irish, *despite* the colour of my skin. That interview was not a nice experience for me; it made me feel "othered", denied my Irishness and prevented me from performing to the best of my ability in the interview. But more than anything, it made me question if I would even want to work in that school that failed to understand that a person of colour can be Irish. It further solidified that what people see ignites their pre-conceived bias and stereotypes and this is negatively affecting Black Irish women's experiences in getting jobs in Ireland.

4.3 Unity is community

In my experience, many who fight for gender equity cannot see how Black Irish women's struggles in the labour force relate to them. For centuries, we, as women, have had to watch our male counterparts advance more quickly in their careers, earn significantly more money than us for similar roles, while we simultaneously struggled to prove the discrimination occurring all around us. The 'box' that women are placed in due to gender inequities and stereotypes becomes even smaller when the women are Black or Brown. When we look closely, we find that many of us from marginalised backgrounds suffer from similar discrimination and negative experiences. The intersectionality ties of gender and race are what unite us and they should motivate us to work together and strive for equity for all.

To address the lack of equity in the labour market for Black Irish women, we need look no further than our neighbouring countries for guidance. We have countries on either side of us that can show us examples of what works and what does not and also what it looks like when nothing is done and marginalised communities continue to experience inequity. The failures of those around us should prompt us as a nation to strive for resources, policy, training, and new strategies to welcome cultural diversity. As a country, we have made advances in bridging gender inequities in the labour force. For those seeking methods to increase ethnic diversity, the same methods should be put in place. Ireland is in its infancy when it comes to our understanding of ethnic diversity but we are in a position to ensure positive change and positive cultural integration as we navigate an ever-changing diverse Ireland.

As women, we know the struggles of discrimination and of the unconscious biases that exist and can hinder our progression in the labour force. No matter what minority group you may belong to, based on class, gender, race, religion or sexual orientation, you know what it feels like to be discriminated against because of it. You know the difficulties behind proving it, the gaslighting that accompanies it and the role it plays in the workplace. It is our intersectional ties that connect us all, reminding us that our experiences are one and the same and so should our support for each other.

Blind screening is one of those ways to improve equitable practices going forward for organisations; unconscious bias training and cultural sensitivity awareness for people at the administrative level. It is crucial for people to become aware of their own unconscious bias, open their eyes and actually see the lack of ethnic diversity in their own companies and organisations and choose to do something about it. Organisations can have all of the policies and strategies in place but if there are no visible changes in ethnic diverse hiring and inclusion, these attempts are futile.

4.4 Visibility in education and the media – Meet Emer O'Neill

I was born in Dublin 1985 to an Irish mother and a Nigerian father. I grew up in Bray, Co. Wicklow at a time when Black Irish people were few and far between. I struggled to see people who looked like me anywhere in my life. Throughout my schooldays all of my teachers and mentors were White. I never had a person of colour teach me, nor had I ever seen a Principal, Deputy Principal or anyone of colour in a leadership position within my educational experience. It was only when I went to America that I saw people of colour in education and leadership roles, and this inspired me to be an educator. I say all of this to highlight the importance of representation and visibility on our young people. The Black Irish community has expanded exponentially since my childhood so the need for diverse representation is more important than ever and a lack of ethnically diverse candidates available for jobs can no longer be used as an excuse for a lack of ethnic diversity in the workplace.

Yet spaces like education have visibly not changed significantly from that of my childhood. We all know the saying 'you've got to see it to be it' used to express the importance of visibility and representation to motivate people to strive for things they may have thought were unattainable to them. An example of which is The Federation of Irish Sports 20x20 women/girls in sport slogan, "If she can see it, she can be it"; a campaign aimed at promoting visibility and equality in women's sport. Many of us in the Black Irish community today have to break down barriers to access places where there has traditionally not been that representation, making it easier for those coming after us. We must make our own path and, in so many places, be the first from our community to do that here in Ireland.

In 2020 during COVID-19, I made my TV debut as 'Múinteoir Emer' on RTE's 'Home School Hub'. This opportunity was life-changing for me. Having never seen anyone that looked like me on my TV screen as a child was damaging. So, to have the opportunity to represent the Black Irish community and be that visible source of identity for children that may have up to that time, felt underrepresented or invisible in Irish society was an incredible joy. The media can change the public's socio-cultural values by generating educational, unbiased, and diverse content. When content represents different groups and voices it can be a source of empathy and civil discourse. External pluralism in the media helps to *normalise* inclusion. When we see people from minority communities front and centre in the media, that visibility humanises their thoughts and ideas that are probably different to ours. It ensures visibility and representation for many underrepresented groups, which can make communities feel like their voices are heard and that they are seen. To achieve internal pluralism within an organisation, underrepresented and marginalised voices must be present (and heard!) at the Board of Management level, in the production and editorial team and in decision-making about content. Achieving diversity and inclusion in the media means the content produced is more accessible and interesting to a wider audience. I challenge you to look at your organisation - *#lookcloser* - and the organisations around you and evaluate how inclusive and diverse you/they truly are both internally and externally. If you are unsatisfied with your findings, then this is your call to action, to ensure that marginalised and underrepresented communities are incorporated in your space, your network, and your organisation. Ní neart go cur le chéile"– With unity, comes strength!

5

Is the lack of equity for Black Irish women intentional?

Tafadzwa Mandiwanza
Consultant paediatric neurosurgeon

5.1 Introduction

I am convinced that there is no equity for Black Irish women in the healthcare sector in Ireland. For example, when I walk around the hospital where I work, there are very few doctors who look like me, although there are definitely more Black, Indian, and Filipino nurses than doctors. In a 2022 Report, more than 90% (68,310) of nurses and midwives registered with NMBI Ireland were women, with 61% of the 2022 registrants educated outside Ireland. This is corroborated by a HSE report where in 2019, just 10% of nursing graduates were men (Hogan, 2023). While half of the doctors graduating from medical schools in Ireland may be female, there is a clear disparity in the ratio of men and women at the higher levels in the healthcare sector. We continue to see more males than females at higher pay grades and this is an area that can be improved upon in Ireland. Black women are rare in hospital medicine and particularly so at consultant level. The ratio of women in senior roles is improving and it is definitely better than it was when I first started my training – but Ireland still has a way to go. I did not see many women working in medicine which I could aspire to when I was a student. There were even fewer in surgery and none of them was Black. I don't think it is intentional that Black Irish women don't have equity in healthcare and I have no evidence. But careers like surgery have always been traditionally the White male domain and not a role many Black women have aspired to, although research by the Royal College of Surgeons may indicate otherwise (RCSI report, 2017). Interestingly, the data showed that while only 7% of surgical consultants were female, 50% of trainees' undergraduate students were female. The lack of equity in medicine starts at the grass roots; Black girls are not encouraged to pursue medicine as a profession; people of migrant descent face a lot of barriers in skills transfer if their skills were learned elsewhere. As there are more second generation Irish born Black women now, I hope that this will change the faces we see entering the healthcare profession in Ireland.

5.2 Black women in medicine have to grow a very thick skin

Based on my experiences of studying and training in Ireland, the biggest challenge that I found as a woman was the expectation that women should achieve the same level, and work the same number of hours as their male colleagues, while at the same time juggling family and childcare commitments. No provision has been put in place to allow for the extra workload of mothers. The alternative for women is to defer raising a family as our male colleagues do not carry the same level of responsibility for caring for young children. A lack of affordable and reliable childcare is a major driver of inequality in the workplace for most women and particularly for Black Irish women. Subsidising childcare for working mothers would go a long way to addressing this. I remember there was a time when my children were very young, with all three attending a full-time crèche and the childcare bill alone was probably more than my mortgage. I had moments when I was discouraged and considered staying at home, certainly it would have been cheaper! I am sure I am not alone and many other working mothers have had the same thought. As a surgical trainee, you are putting in more than 80 hours a week of training and as a mother, you have to balance the time left with your children. There is so much guilt that comes with not seeing your children as much as other mothers do. It is very difficult, and many women have changed their specialties in medicine as a result to those less time demanding roles.

There is definitely still a lot of work to be done in encouraging female doctors to pursue surgical specialties. Unlike many other Irish women, most Black women in Ireland are immigrants or refugees and don't have the 'village' (their wider family) support. I was blessed that my sister-in-law managed to come over and live with us. She took on a lot of the childcare needs that I had at the time. There are places that I have lived in Ireland where I did not even know my neighbours! This is partly because I am shy, and because I don't get a lot of opportunities to interact with people outside of work because of the long hours. Like other Black Irish women, I feel a bit more isolated than I would be if I was living in my country of birth. The solution might be as simple as Black women needing to be a little bit more outgoing or as complex as the community around them should embrace them more. But it's an isolation issue as well. It is very hard.

My husband, who is also a doctor, was training at the same time as I was. Culturally and traditionally many of us Black women are raised to defer to men and were told that our place is in the home. It's a challenge for Black Irish women to break out of these built-in stereotypes, so many may not try. So, our culture can also act as a barrier to workplace equity.

These are some of the challenges for any woman pursuing a medical career but I think as a Black woman, there is the added challenge of pre-conceived bias. People rarely assume I'm a doctor when they first meet me. Some even refuse to acknowledge that I am a doctor even after I tell them. For some colleagues, I am already considered to be an inferior doctor from the outset. Black women in medicine, in particular, have to grow a very thick skin. I have had to learn not to be too sensitive about the bias I face day to day. My particular mantra is that I love to surprise people! I love it even more when they realise that I am good at what I do! These underlying biases and day-to-day challenges with patients and colleagues could make entering this profession unappealing.

5.3 What do we need for Black women to have equity?

Encouraging Black Irish women and leading by example is a good first step in working towards achieving equity. Excelling and persisting in kindness goes a long way towards dispelling or starting to unravel the hidden bias that is there. Of course, it will take time and probably a few generations before Black women in Ireland are considered as equals to White women, but in the mean time we have a standard to keep. The visibility of women, especially Black Irish women in medical professions will encourage younger women coming through, that medicine is possible as a career. Black women who have achieved and attained at high levels encourage the young ones as they come up. Me being in my role lets the young ones know that it's achievable. That while, yes, you may be Black and yes, you may be a woman – it is not a limitation to what they can do.

From an employer's perspective, my experiences suggest I would never get a job because I was Black and a woman. Rather, I got to where I am today *despite* being a Black woman. In my opinion, it is harmful for favour to be shown to a person because of their ethnicity and gender. It is usually misconstrued and used against Black people as well as fuelling the bias of those around them. We need to balance encouraging Black Irish women into work spaces but allowing them to get there on their own merit and this is a fine line to tread. The environment I work in right now is very inclusive and they are striving to improve in diversity and inclusion. Ireland is a very different place from how it was when I first arrived. It is definitely improving but we are still far off being a melting pot of cultures and diversity.

5.4 Black Irish women engaging in extra work in society

Unfortunately, I have been so focused on getting to this point in my career and making things work in my own household that I have not done any activism or community work. Many other Black Irish women are involved in community activism because we are proud of who we are and what we can achieve. We want to be heard and it is important for us to be seen and engage with the wider community. As newcomers it helps us to develop a sense of belonging. It is also a way of improving the situation for our children. For myself, community volunteering and activism is something that I would be interested in getting involved in over the next few years. I have now reached the point in my career where I can finally breathe a little bit and there is now the chance for me to carve out some time to do things like that.

5.5 Dr. Tafadzwa Mandiwanza, the Black Irish paediatric neurosurgeon

I was born in Zimbabwe, which is in Southern Africa. I am the first of three children and I have two younger brothers. In Shona culture, I am not considered the first-born child in the family, my brother is. Growing up, I always had a strong sense of trying to stand out in my family and maybe this was partly because I was rebelling against the cultural norms that told me that I was less important than a male child. I always wanted to study medicine, apparently from the age of three (!) according to my parents, who have been very supportive in getting me to this point. I completed my A-Levels at home in Zimbabwe, after which I applied for a place at University College Cork, which I fortunately got accepted to. I had always lived at home. I did not go to boarding schools like my brothers did. So, coming to Ireland alone was a seminal point in my development. I had a little bit of independence and I could discover who I

really was but I always kept my focus on medical school. I was always conscious of the fact that if I failed, I would be letting a whole clan down. I got through medical school and got into surgical training. I am a very practical person. I was that child who would fix a bike when I was growing up. I am very good with my hands. I had just completed basic surgical training when I had my first baby. I had her and then two years later, her sister came along and then two years after that their brother came along. You can say it was a busy 6 years of babies with a lot happening in our household.

Eventually I got accepted to the higher surgical training scheme and neurosurgery was my passion. I could not imagine being any other type of surgeon or doing anything else for work. I worked between Beaumont Hospital and Cork during that time. Paediatrics neurosurgery was my main interest, simply because I had two mentors who were very interested in my career, my pathway and who were very supportive and encouraging. I went to Great Ormond Street, London for a year of Fellowship which was an amazing experience. It is ranked in the top three paediatric hospitals in the world. So, it was an amazing experience to even be there but it was nice to see how their systems operate. One of the best things I discovered when I was in London is that Dublin was not that far behind what they do and I thought that was amazing. Because you always hear people complaining about our health system and about the waiting times but don't forget that we are at the cutting edge of what is happening in the world. We are doing things as well as, if not better, than our neighbours and North America. I found that a positive and heartening discovery. I always wanted to come back to Dublin and fortunately the position opened up and I was successful in getting the job. So here I am back in Ireland again!

So, what about Zimbabwe, the country that I love, but that makes me sad too. The way things have changed over the last 20 and more years is disheartening. The political situation there is not great. The economic situation is even worse. The health system is struggling to say the least. It is sad that I am not living there. It is sad that I am not bringing up my children there as I used to think I would. As a mother, you have to do what's best and look at what's best for your children and I think being in Ireland is what's best for my family.

References

NMBI State of the Register 2022 1st June 2022. Available at; https://www.nmbi.ie/NMBI/media/NMBI/NMBI-State-of-the-Register-2022.pdf. Accessed 23 January, 2024.

Hogan Jan, Sat Feb 18 2023. Amongst women: Why are there so few men in caring roles? https://www.irishtimes.com/health/2023/02/11/amongst-women-why-are-there-so-few-men-in-caring-roles/#:~:text=According%20to%20the%20HSE%2C%20fewer,10%20per%20cent%20are%20men

RCSI 2017 report. Progress: Promoting Gender Equality In Surgery Report of the Gender Diversity Short Life Working Group. Available here: https://www.rcsi.com/impact/details/2020/02/addressing-the-gender-gap-in-surgery

6
Black Irish women are denied equity within the workplace

Dr. Phil Mullen
Assistant Professor of Black Studies

6.1 Introduction

I am firm in my belief that Black employees as a group do not have equity. This dovetails with a broader perspective, which highlights that women as a group still do not have equity in the labour market. PwC's *Women in Work Index 2023* shows that the gender pay gap is 6.9%, leading the authors to conclude with this bleak assessment that <u>If progress towards gender equality at work continues at its historical rate, an 18-year-old woman starting today will not see pay equality in her working life</u>. So, when we examine the intersectional implications of gender (shown above) and race on Black Irish women, it is obvious that Black Irish women do not have equity in the labour market in Ireland. While evidence supports this contention, (European Union Agency for Fundamental Rights, 2023; Joseph, 2020), as well as anecdotally within the community, we still face a considerable challenge in making our case as we must counter the false argument that the lack of participation by Black women is just a game of numbers. The argument is that there are not enough qualified Black women to fill the available positions. This is a false argument but this is not a surprise, given the discriminatory nature of much of the current discourse towards Black people in Ireland. Unfortunately, it is an argument which finds much purchase in Irish public opinion. But research shows us how Black women are actually positioned within the labour markets in Ireland. So, it is not a question of lack of numbers, but rather it is the grim reality of the devaluation of the qualifications of Black women which leads to Black Irish women being underrepresented within the labour market.

I say 'grim' above as the real-life impacts of this devaluation of the Black female can result in egregious acts. I know personally that some people within academia, some Black women, have had their qualifications challenged while teaching within the classroom by white students who are seemingly unable or unwilling to accept their presence in such a professional setting. One Black female academic had a White Irish student who stood up and challenged the legitimacy of her role as a lecturer and demanded in the public forum of a well-attended lecture hall to know what her qualifications were. From my own research, I regularly encounter Black women who work in healthcare settings who are challenged in a similar manner as to their suitability to occupy this perceived 'White space', and of course these impacts on their ability to do their job. It impacts on their self-esteem. And this refusal to accept the Black body within what many people seem to view as 'White-only professional spaces' has played a not insignificant role in denying equity within the workplace.

As a working Black academic in the White space that is an Irish university (and let's be fair with a name such as mine) I, like Emer O'Neill, consistently encounter a phenomenon I term in my research as 'unexpected Irishness', where Black bodies, Black lived experiences, and Black knowledge(s) pop up in imagined White spaces, discourses and episteme. The unexpectedness of my voice, hailing as it does from this small Black body is then forced to deal with the awkwardness, and do the work of justifying my existence in a White space. I am forced to almost interrogate the essentialised identities, racial hierarchies, and conflicting world views of being marked as 'Black in Ireland', as well as their resulting structural manifestations in terms of education and job opportunities.

6.2 Are Black Irish women at the back of the bus or driving the bus?

There are several elements to the challenge of Black Irish women accessing equity. The inherent structural and systemic elements which impact Black Irish women in the workplace begins early, at getting their CVs past the less than welcoming eyes of HR. Research has revealed a concerning trend where the CVs of Black women may go unnoticed or be rejected outright for roles demanding advanced cognitive skills. The exoticization of African names and disqualification based on a bias against qualifications awarded by African universities are likely to be factors in this rejection.

If they successfully get past the HR gatekeepers and through the interview process to actually landing a job, they are then faced with dealing with a workplace which inevitably has an anti-Black bias leading to racialisation of these working women. So, they can expect their hair, food, language, accent, and names to be interrogated once they eventually get access to the labour market. People come up to touch their hair. People complaining about their food. Questions as about their competency are based on their 'non-Irish-sounding accents'. In a multitude of ways, their identities within the Irish labour market are contested in a way which challenges their right to be there. What should be commonplace, everyday workplace interactions and discourse instead become struggles for legitimacy and the right to take up space within the workplace.

Experiencing struggles like this to establish a person's legitimacy will invariably have a negative impact on that person's sense of self-esteem, and make them feel undervalued in the workplace and leads to one of the more grievous forms of lack of equity within the workplace in Ireland. The harm caused to one's sense of self within the workplace prevents the establishment of social networks. Black Irish women are less likely to build up social networks within the workplace due to systemic issues like unconscious biases, cultural differences, and historical patterns of exclusion. We have to remember that Black as phenotype must be understood to encompass a broader range of perceivable characteristics beyond skin colour, such as hair texture, facial features, and body type. Phenotype transcends what Frantz Fanon called the materiality of the body (Fanon, 1952) and also may be precipitated by socio-cultural, linguistic, and psychological markers (e.g., names, accent, clothing, etc.) or exclusionary barriers can hinder the formation of connections for Black women, which can stand in the way of career advancement, mentorship, and professional support. In a homogenous workplace, diversity-related issues may also contribute to a sense of isolation for Black Irish women, making it harder to establish meaningful relationships. Overcoming these obstacles requires a concerted effort from both individuals and organisations to promote inclusivity, cultural awareness, and equal opportunities within the workplace. However, Black women in the workplace often face a more insidious problem – they can't mention anything relating to 'race issues' because even mentioning could attract a charge of racism, and 'talking about' race is 'considered an act of war' (Williams, 1995: 40). Without the support of such networks, it is considerably more difficult to build up the social capital required to progress within work roles and within the institution itself. This has the effect of stopping Black women from progressing, thus slowing down their trajectory. In some cases, this actually means that they do not even have a trajectory in terms of getting promotions or leadership positions. Black Irish women often find themselves, to take an old phrase, at the back of the bus when they are actually capable of driving the bus.

6.3 Addressing Anti-Black tendencies within the recruitment sector in Ireland

One of the first things that needs to be done is to rigorously implement the equality legislation that already exists. Policies are all well and good, but the proof of the pudding is in the sort of implementation that would make Black Irish women feel secure that they will not be victimised or be the ultimate losers if they complain. For example, in my field, I'm thinking of Sara Ahmed's book Complaint, which focuses on the stories of individuals navigating formal complaint processes in higher education. By examining how people perceive the same environment differently, Ahmed unveils the inner workings of institutions. Ahmed advocates for a feminist understanding of complaint politics, challenging the idea that institutions are immutable and unchangeable entities, highlighting complaints as powerful refusals to accept the status quo.

It is no great revelation to any Black women who has applied for a job or worked in the Irish labour market that there are not only racist, but determinedly anti-Black tendencies within the recruitment sector in Ireland and within some workplaces, which need to be addressed. And the best manner, in fact, the only manner in which to do this successfully, is to 'address' said tendencies through the implementation of robust equality legislation, with definable metrics of measuring success in achieving greater equity as well as punitive measures to ensure compliance. Incentivising more inclusive practices through different schemes, tougher sanctions or possibly public recognition of good practice can encourage companies to proactively address inequities. Research initiatives should be supported to collect and analyse data on workplace demographics and challenges faced by Black women on an ongoing basis.

This is an area where I think the employer must really pitch in and do their part to create a safe space for Black Irish women where they are experiencing intersectional elements of oppression, discrimination, and bias within the workforce. As my experience is within the public sector, I will speak to that. EDI (equity, diversity, and inclusion) in public sector institutions has to have more meaning than just box ticking. Inclusion and diversity are elements of social justice that must be meaningfully implemented. The Public Sector Equality and Human Rights Duty legislation, as part of Section 42 of the Irish Human Rights and Equality Act 2014, needs to be better known by members of minority groups who require protection under it. This legislation states that public body employers, such as universities, hospitals or schools are obliged to tackle discrimination. They have to promote equality and they have to protect human rights.

This is a significant piece of legislation which protects vulnerable people in the public sector labour market and which could change the career trajectory of many Black Irish women within the workforce. What appeals to me is that it is not a 'one and done operation', because it means that every year when preparing annual reports and strategic plans, public bodies must assess, address, and report on what progress they are making in the area of EDI. I would advocate for similar levels of accountability and transparency in every organisation, private as well as public. This approach would certainly make a marked difference to the experiences of Black women in the workplace in Ireland.

6.4 Black Irish women act as catalysts for change

Most of us Black women have to do more to achieve the same as our White peers. I would like to briefly examine one form of extra work that I have had to do all of my life, which I would confidently assume my White contemporaries never had to consider in their own lives. I think anybody who has been racialised is forced into doing the extra work of being 'raced' not by choice but by necessity and for self-preservation. Phenotype is a master status for many of us, as the attribution of 'raced' is forced upon us and obliges us to take a stand, usually from quite a young age. So, even as a child, I was very conscious of not being like everybody else. I couldn't be anything other than conscious as my life in Ireland pre-dates the Celtic Tiger and my phenotype was even more isolating then than it would be in 2024. And that isolation, if I think of my working life back in the 1980s and early 1990s, was aggravated by the daily racial intimidation I suffered while at work, and often on the way to work in the mornings and while heading home in the evenings and from work. My sense of being made different by those around me made me conscious of the discrimination and inequity that was prevalent in my life, such as the limited opportunities I had – my first jobs were as a kitchen porter and office cleaner.

One of two things can happen when you have to endure being racialised in such a White space. Some people may look inward and perversely locate the source of the problem in themselves. Others, like me, look outward and challenge the behaviour of the society around me. But to successfully look out, one has to do the work and achieve a certain racial literacy. One also needs a community, which also entails a great deal of work. I began to look out and to explore the world more, turning my gaze toward America, looking to the UK, finding writers who spoke to my experience. I began a journey to learn about race and racism and the impact of racialisation on me and the small number of Black Irish women like me who began to find each other in the mid-1990s. I began to work to find my community. I also began to work for my community. In 1994, I joined the African and Migrant Women's Association – a collective of African and Caribbean women, and Black Irish and Black British women – coming together for mutual support in Ireland. I also found my sense of isolation being pierced by the community offered by the organisation, Harmony. I took up a role in a new organisation called the African Cultural Project and made some life-long friends with the Black African women with whom I worked.

What I learnt is that it is important to be involved at whatever level you can and wherever you feel comfortable but to *be involved*. Women are historically catalysts for change, they drive movements – we see it happening in Iran, where women led and men followed, sometimes reluctantly. African and Black women join social movements driven by their shared experiences and commitment. But mostly they do so to make things better and to protect their children, and other younger versions of themselves from the experiences they have endured. For me as a Black woman and as a mother, the real purpose of this extra work is to try and make it easier for each successive generation of Black women. This is why many Black women choose to take on this particular form of extra work.

6.5 Meet Dr Phil Mullen, racialised as 'Black' or 'Mixed race' in a White world

I was born in Dublin. My father was a Nigerian student in Ireland and my mother was a pale, red-headed Irish woman ... the archetypal Irish female. They were not married when I was born, so I was placed in an industrial school. My proximity to Whiteness was total but I was consistently told that I did not belong. To be racialised as 'Black' in a White world or perhaps, latterly, 'Mixed race' is a heavy burden, full to the brim of damaging stereotypes and it is what I encountered every day during my formative years. It had a big impact on how I saw myself, on my sense of belonging, whether I was Irish or whether I was in fact this entity called 'Black'; I wasn't sure as a young person what that meant or what kind of an identity I had. Trying to understand the processes of racialisation has been challenging. I left school initially with no qualifications but like so many Black Irish women, I wasn't content. Even after a bachelor's degree, a master's degree and a PhD, I am still looking for answers every day.

After a working life in the NGO sector, I now find myself lecturing in Trinity College Dublin. In some ways teaching Black Studies is the culmination of those early experiences of not being allowed to belong. Certainly, my desire to encourage other Black academics starting out in whatever discipline they are studying, comes from mining my own experiences. It also comes from recognising that, no matter how elevated the rung of the ladder on which you perch, you didn't get there yourself but were helped by those who form your community. Equally, that perch needs to be made wider and strong enough to accommodate all those who are coming behind and deserve to rise as high as they can. And let me tell you, there is a generation of younger Black Irish women coming up who will not take as long as I did to raise their voices in opposition to being told 'you do not belong!' I'm happy to be in the role I am in because it allows me to witness, and maybe even play a small part in influencing, this new engagement between Blackness and Irishness.

References

Ahmed, S. (2021). *Complaint!* Durham: Duke University Press.

European Union Agency for Fundamental Rights (2023). *Being Black in the EU: Experiences of people of African descent*. Luxembourg: Publications Office of the European Union.

Fanon, F. (1952). *Black Skin, White Masks*. New York: Grove Press.

Joseph, E. (2020). *Critical Race Theory and Inequality in the Labour Market: Racial Stratification in Ireland* (1st ed.). Manchester: Manchester University Press.

PwC (2023). Women in Work Index 2023.
https://www.pwc.ie/reports/women-in-work-index.html

Williams P (1995) *The Rooster's Egg: The Persistence of Prejudice*. Cambridge, MA: Harvard University Press.

7

Discrimination and negative attitudes towards Black Irish women maintain inequity

Dr Salome Mbugua
CEO of AkiDwA, The Migrant Women's Network Ireland

7.1 Introduction

From my experience and from the experience of many organisations that we work with at AkiDwA, it is clear that we are very far from achieving equity for Black women in Ireland. Research shows that the majority of migrant women, and in particular Black Irish women are highly educated compared to White Irish women, but their chances of accessing jobs in the labour market, particularly those jobs that match their qualifications is very, very far from being achieved. We have a lot of women who participate in training, they go to college and better themselves but when you look at their equality of outcome after spending years in training, it is not there. They hardly manage to access employment in fields that match their qualifications even when they have studied in universities in Ireland. For them to get jobs that match their qualifications, it is still so hard. There are a lot of issues including discrimination which is formed by negative attitudes and stereotypes about women of African descent. And my organisation in particular has researched these issues. As Black women living in Ireland in the 21st century, we are very far from achieving this equity.

7.2 Ignored credentials during recruitment affects Black Irish women

It is actually very sad because Black Irish women have a lot of difficulty in trying to get equity in the labour market. When we talk about Black Irish women – or people of African descent to be more specific – all of the research shows that the majority of these women experience a lot of discrimination when trying to access services; our report *on Black Women in the Irish Labour Market* found some key challenges (Hegarty, 2007). AkiDwA ('Akina Dada wa Africa') is a network of migrant women (90% are African Irish) in Ireland. The majority of these women don't even find out about job opportunities and even when they do, they are often excluded from activities and existing opportunities. And when they apply for these jobs, they are not even called for an interview or sometimes their applications are not acknowledged. We know that the majority are highly qualified, with bachelor's degrees and master's degrees and many have PhDs. When they apply for jobs that match their areas of their specialisation, some of them don't get called for interviews. And some don't ever hear back from the organisations they applied to. This is an indication that there are a lot of challenges. Discrimination is a major concern. I want to say that very clearly because we have researched this subject area. And many instances of discrimination have been reported to us at AkiDwA.

7.3 Prompt action is needed for Black and African women to have equity

We need to come up with various actions, and quickly because this group have been particularly discriminated against and ignored for so long. Additionally, many reports highlighting what needs to be done have been published to little or no effect. Black women need to be supported to reach their full potential. They are hardworking, resilient, and very responsible. Quite often they participate and engage in community-level activities through voluntary work, even during times of personal difficulty. It is time the government came up with measures which include positive actions to address the particular challenges faced by Black Irish women, especially to help them to get access the labour market, engage in decision-making, and participate in society more. African Irish women are primary carers of their families – and many of them are parenting their families alone. Our organisation – AkiDwA has conducted a lot of research, published position papers, and engaged with Government departments (www.akidwa.ie). We are always appearing before the various subcommittees in the Dáil (Irish government), discussing Black women's experiences and the challenges they are facing in getting jobs and access to justice in the face of discrimination. Black Irish women like White Irish women struggle with issues of domestic violence. What we encounter is that no one, organisation or department wants to take responsibility or take clear actions to help with this issue.

Black women are not a homogenous group, but they are being left behind in many areas, so an assessment of the gaps and challenges faced by these women is needed. We need to come up with real actions that will help them. Working with other organisations and using our inspirational Black Irish role models is a good way of encouraging and motivating people. In Ireland at the moment, it is very, very difficult to see Black women at different levels of decision-making, to see them working in politics, or in professional jobs. We really need strategies to support Black Irish women and to promoting equity for them in the workplace. This can however only be done if the State takes the action itself. Affirmative action would be one of them because if the start of equality cannot be achieved, and we are talking about equity now and we have not even approached real equality for Black Irish women. I think it is just a shame. But this is a song that has been going on for a long time and we really need to act on it and see changes. We can look at how to support women more and in particular Black Irish women.

We also should be engaging with organisations that are working with these women at the local level. Ireland has 26 counties. We need to reach out to all the women around the country. Black Irish women in Dublin are better off as they are closer to most of the services, which are all in Dublin. In some counties, women can't access certain essential services. For example, AkiDwA is a lead organisation on female genital mutilation (FGM), and women are travelling long distances from Cork to Dublin to be treated for issues relating to FGM at the Rotunda hospital, which is really unacceptable, especially for some who are living with a very traumatic kind of situation where travelling long distances for treatment can be uncomfortable and exacerbates the situation. The Irish government and the state need to work with local groups, hospitals and other frontline services to provide wrap-around services that are culturally appropriate.

7.4 Black Irish women transform society by their voluntary community work

I can almost say categorically that the people who are volunteering in this country more than anyone else are Black Irish women. Quite often, they don't seek to be financially compensated for the extra work they do. They don't do it to receive praise. I think voluntary work for Black Irish women is just part of us, it's in our genes. Many Black African Irish women volunteer in community groups around the country. More importantly, there are many groups and organisations that are led by Black Irish women in Ireland. They come up with solutions and ways to solve some of the local problems they are experiencing. If they weren't doing that, we would be talking of a different Ireland, a place where Black women and their families would feel lost. Black Irish women are carrying a lot of the weight through their sacrifice and their struggle as they continue to volunteer. They are contributing a lot and they are transforming Ireland. We are some of those women. My organisation, AkiDwA, is one of those organisations that runs through the work of many volunteers; we are trying to work with women who have been abused, and those who have suffered in other ways. Black Irish women don't look into how they can make gains out of the volunteering work; they support and transform the society that they are living in now without waiting for any awards or rewards that may come their way. And usually, their work is being quietly organised and it is not really noticed or seen.

7.5 Dr. Salome Mbugua is a BIFFO – a Beautiful, Intelligent Female from Offaly

It is very hard to discuss about oneself. I don't know what I can call myself because I want to identify with Ireland, but quite often, I am reminded that I

am not Irish. When I hear and see that and the contribution that I am making in this country, it makes me sad. I call myself a 'BIFFO' - a Beautiful, Intelligent, Female from Offaly and people laugh. And this is because I am beautiful as you can see but also very intelligent. I am transforming Ireland every time I sit on the different advisory groups, boards and committees that I am involved in, including the Irish Human Right and Equality Commission. It is there that I make my contribution to transform our vibrant society into a better Ireland. I arrived in this beautiful country 27 years ago. I didn't sit down and wait for things to be done for me. I have actually been transforming Ireland one day at a time with the work that I do. I completed most of my studies in Ireland. I was recently awarded my PhD degree from Trinity College Dublin. I work in an organisation called AkiDwA that I founded in 2001. We presently employ 12 staff. We are providing employment as we try to transform Ireland in a significant way where everybody will be valued, treated with respect, and dignity and feel protected whatever they do. I came from a small village in Kenya and both my parents have passed now but I know that they are happy about the work that I do. Because I am here to transform. I am here to do good and that's me.

References

Hegarty, F.M. (2007) Black African Women in the Irish Labour Market. AkiDwA. Ireland.

https://emn.ie/publications/black-african-women-in-the-irish-labour-market/

8

Black women in Irish society are the 'other'

Winifred Ikhine Akinyemi
Civil servant, Department of Foreign Affairs

8.1 Introduction

I love the word 'equity'. I first encountered it as an 18-year-old law student in Nigeria, my country of birth. I was told that equity mitigates the harshness of the common law. That idea has always stayed with me. My understanding is that when the law and policies create hardship for people especially those who are vulnerable, marginalised, or underrepresented, equity should step in and provide remedies to the wrongs based on the particular situation of those affected. Equity represents the voice of conscience and fairness. Black Irish women as a particular group is not recognized in Ireland. There is no provision for equity to be applied to our particular circumstances or challenges. Equity for Black Irish women does not exist and it is not just in the labour market but everywhere. Black women in Irish society are 'the other' and the general laws are made for the benefit of indigenous White citizens. This is because there is no understanding or consideration of the challenges or experiences that must be addressed for Black Irish women to compete with others in Ireland and achieve their potential.

8.2 Lack of equity for Black Irish women in the labour market is a triple whammy

One of the problems Black people faced in the past was the non-recognition of their educational qualifications, obtained in our countries of origin. When I first arrived in Ireland over 20 years ago, I was the victim of this. My legal qualifications were not recognized and so I had to reskill. While nowadays the qualifications of new immigrants to Ireland are recognized (NARIC – Quality &

Qualifications Ireland), this still does not translate into recognition in actually getting a job. The non-recognition of our qualifications in the past for people like me certainly has repercussions in my day-to-day life. The fact that my skills and work experience were also basically not recognized certainly was damaging and it prevented me from using those skills to contribute to Irish society. To mitigate the injustice we encountered, many of us have spent unaccounted for years reskilling to acquire a recognized third-level qualification in Ireland. In addition to suffering the indignity of having work experience totally expunged from our records, we spent years struggling to catch up with our pre-migration professional positions and relatively high socio-economic status. This injustice is in addition to the other microaggressions experienced by Black Irish women based on their gender and race.

8.3 We need to invite Black women to the decision-making tables

Black Irish women can only have equity in Ireland if their previous lives, including skills and work experiences, are fully acknowledged and recognized. I had to start afresh in terms of education and work experience when I came to Ireland. I had to go back to study for another bachelor's degree, followed by a Master's degree. It was not just the educational level, but also our capacity to competently complete tasks and duties is not recognised. This set me back many years. One of the reasons it is not recognized I believe is because we are not sitting at the table in mainstream or government spaces where decisions that affect our lives are being made. This is why as a civil servant; I have made it my priority to contribute to the inclusion and diversity initiatives in the sector to ensure that there is representation of minority groups.

The real question is, how can Black people, including Black women sit at the decision-making tables? How can our situations and experiences be considered, when decisions are being made? How can we be part of the conversations? Because we need to be part of the decision-making spaces for the outcomes to include ways to address our particular set of challenges. To encourage more Black women to work in the civil service here, we need another competition like the one used for Clerical Officer competition for Ukrainian nationals in 2023. It successfully provided immediate visibility within government spaces. Another solution is to improve diversity in interview panels so that interviewers have a better understanding of the life experiences and cultures of the diverse candidates in front of them.

8.4 Extra community work by Black Irish women is to ensure minority voices are represented

I was having a conversation about representation with a colleague the other day and I started listing my voluntary work commitments, and needless to say my colleague was left open-mouthed! As I explained to him, it's not that I am heading for sainthood, but the constant lack of representation at work and at home means that a person who wants to make an impact will have no choice but to take on many voluntary roles. So, we end up doing our job, volunteering for extra work at work, and doing voluntary work in our local community after work in an effort to ensure better representation and to facilitate the minority voices to be better heard.

I volunteer as a convenor of the Multicultural Working Group, which draws on the wealth of voices from across the Department of Foreign Affairs (DFA) to highlight its diverse nature. The group champions and celebrates diversity, including ethnic diversity in the workplace. I am used to supporting in spaces where I am the only Black person. At times it is like I have to represent an entire race or an entire continent!

In the Lucan-Adamstown area of South Dublin County Council, where I have lived for 16 years, I volunteer in a number of committees and companies. You find that it is always the same three people who end up working to organise things in the community. And like the saying goes, "If you want to get something done, ask a busy person". It is the same Black woman who is doing everything, volunteering at work, in her community, in her children's school and even in her religious space. I now truly understand the saying that you have to work four times harder than other people, because it is actually true. We are always taking on so many responsibilities and trying to ensure that other people are included and not left behind.

8.6 'The Climb'–navigating my way up the ladder–Winifred Ikhine Akinyemi

My long journey to my current role in Ireland started with not getting recognition for my legal qualifications and having to accept jobs that I was overqualified for. I would still have been in that situation, but now, I have been able to integrate into mainstream Irish society and become a full time, permanent Irish Civil Servant. I call this part of my journey *"The Climb"*. It is really like a very difficult uphill climb where I am constantly trying to develop

myself, trying to get to a level similar to my pre-migration professional life. It is a continuous struggle and it is also the reason I persist and never give up.

My journey in the Irish labour market has been very insightful, I continue to reflect on and learn from it. I first arrived in Ireland over 20 years ago, in 2004, with a law degree, as a qualified solicitor from Nigeria. I had 13 years' experience of working as a lawyer after being called to the Bar and 10 years' of work experience in the financial sector in Lagos. My last big assignment was coordinating the Initial Public Offer (IPO) on the floor of the Nigerian Stock Exchange (NSE). With all of these achievements behind me, in Ireland, I confidently applied for jobs in large organisations like HSBC, A&L Goodbody, Standard Life, etc. These were the organisations I felt qualified to be employed in. I was invited for some interviews but I never got a job in that sector. With great sadness, I decided to abandon the legal job market and look at other areas for employment. Making this decision was heartbreaking because all I wanted to be in life was a lawyer.

To help with my job hunting, in 2007 I signed up for a 6-week employment support programme, which led to a paid FÁS traineeship as an administrator in an NGO called Spirasi, which supports newly arrived asylum seekers who had been victims of torture. My colleagues in the health information team were legal and medical professionals and I enjoyed working with the outreach team, visiting asylum reception centres and facilitating information sessions with the residents.

Following the traineeship, I began working as a support worker in a mental health project for asylum seekers funded by the European Refugee Fund (ERF) with match funding from the Health Service Executive (HSE) Social Inclusion Unit. My work experience and my performance at Spirasi gave me an advantage over other candidates. This made me feel really good, knowing that my hard work had not been in vain. My new role required me to be based in

Portlaoise for 3 out of 5 days, providing support to a community of people seeking asylum and living in a direct provision accommodation I worked in Co. Laois for 3 days and reported to the Dublin office for 2 days. My daughter had just started junior infants and childcare was the biggest challenge for me. Luckily for me the salary was good and I could afford childcare for my daughter. Commuting from Dublin to Portlaoise was another challenge but my determination kept me going. I had a good experience in this role, and I was able to showcase and enhance my skills. Unfortunately, in 2010 we had a recession in the country and I became unemployed. I went back to job hunting but had no luck for months. For 6 months, I lived on my savings and could not bear the stigma of going on the dole. I remember my Irish friends saying that I must be crazy for not signing up for social welfare payments. They explained that I was entitled to it and that my taxes from previous employment contributed to the government finances. Unfortunately, I was having none of that, growing up in a society that did not provide social protection would not let me understand. I have also been socialised in my middle-class family in Nigeria to view a handout as something shameful and disgraceful.

Being unemployed gave me the opportunity to go back to education and upskill myself. Since I had a third level degree from Nigeria (which the QQI at that time recognized as the equivalent of an Irish level 8 qualification), I should have applied for a master's degree (level 9), but I could not afford to pay the third level non-EU fees, which was applicable to my immigration Stamp 4 status. The policy at the time excluded me from benefiting from third level educational support because of my non-Irish nationality. My previously paid taxes when working was not taken into account; it also did not matter that I was a single parent of a 6-year-old Irish child. The many hours of unpaid volunteering in my community were not considered either. At the time, I wondered about the fairness of this policy, which did not make any provision for the most marginalised and did not prioritise the people who were lagging farthest behind first. Eventually, in 2008, I started a degree programme in Development Studies at Kimmage Development Studies Centre (KDSC), which is now part of Maynooth University. How I managed to pay the €10,000 fees for the programme was some sort of a miracle. I came across a scholarship advertised by KDSC, I applied, and to my surprise I was successful. After my study in 2012, 20 years after my last academic pursuit at the Nigerian law school, I graduated with first class honours. This was another surprise due to the challenges of single parenting and low finances as a student.

My excellent grades made way for my next employment opportunity as a part-time external development facilitator at the Irish Aid Centre. Initially I was an independent service provider, I had to organise my own taxes and the hours were tricky. Things got better when I became an employee of KDSC and the terms improved. The part-time work suited me, I was able to drop off and collect my child from primary school. Working in the DFA environment, I learned a lot and with my legal background I decided that if I worked hard, I could get a civil service job, working to implement Ireland's foreign policy in DFA.

I started applying for jobs in DFA, and when I saw that the requirement of the JPI programme at DFA was a master's degree, I applied for a master's programme at UCD. In 2014, as a single mother, I worked part-time in the Irish Aid Centre and completed my full-time master's degree in International Development and graduated with a 2.1 grade. I immediately applied for the next JPI programme and was successful. I was placed on a panel for 1 year until September 2016, and then I was assigned to a unit based in Limerick. This meant relocating to Limerick or at the least having a physical presence in Limerick from Monday to Friday. I had a 12-year-old child who was starting secondary school. Luckily, I had been proactive and had secured her admission into a 5-day boarding school. Quitting was just not an option for me regardless of the challenges. For the next 4 months, my daughter travelled on the school bus to Kilkenny on a Sunday evening while I drove to Limerick and we both made our way back to Dublin on Fridays. I initially stayed with friends while searching for accommodation in a shared house or apartment. This proved to be extremely difficult so I moved into an Air B&B, which was expensive. Eventually, things got worse and I was on the verge of quitting. Luckily, for me, my director intervened and I was able to work from Dublin. Those 2 years provided me with a great opportunity for developing my skills and proving my abilities.

During the JPI, I applied for different civil service roles when they were advertised but I was unsuccessful. The numerical assessment tests was my biggest challenge but I persisted and eventually I easily passed the tests and got invitations to the next stages including interviews. After the JPI, with support from my internal networks in DFA, I returned to my previous external service role in the Irish Aid Centre and worked there from Sept 2018 to March 2020. In 2019 I applied for a Clerical Officer (CO) role in the hope of eventually getting a permanent civil service position and working my way up. It turned out to be the best decision I ever made and I was successful. Shortly after COVID-19 struck, workers whose jobs were affected received social welfare support. That would have been my fate but luckily, I had started work in April 2020. As we have observed with many Black people of African descent in Ireland, I too was overqualified for that grade by very many academic levels, working years of experience and competencies. I however gave the job my all and focussed on my long-term goal to work my way up and use every opportunity to develop myself. In 2020 I applied for the Higher Executive Officer (HEO) competition as a CO and made it to the final interview stage, which was very encouraging. I was promoted to Executive Officer (EO) grade in August 2022 and to HEO grade in April 2023.

In conclusion, success in the labour market for Black women in Ireland is an uphill task and state support is required to enable marginalised, underrepresented minority groups like Black Irish women and all people of African descent to be at the decision-making tables. We need to be intentional about having specific competitions for Black women and other minority groups, similar to what was done for the Ukrainians. Diversity on interview boards is necessary for a better connection between the interviewers and the candidate.

9
Equity doesn't play well for the Black Irish woman; it hasn't worked for me

Dr Loveth Owhor
Medical researcher and bioresource technologist

9.1 Introduction

It is a well-known fact that Black Irish women in Ireland do not have equity in the labour market. It is something that we all shy away from talking about, especially with other female colleagues who are not Black. If I review my work history in Ireland, I cannot say in all fairness that I have experienced equity in the labour market. I am a Black woman who holds a PhD. I started searching for a job that befits my academic qualification after I graduated from my doctoral studies. This was very challenging. While I was in college studying for my PhD, I taught undergraduate students in the School of Medicine. However, when I graduated it was difficult to get a job in the academic sector. I applied but I got so many rejections. I agreed to get a job that was lower than my highest academic qualification with a firm. While working in that firm, job openings became available for staff, and I happily applied for a particular position because I met the required qualification and, on several occasions, I had deputised for that position on a voluntary basis. I was well versed on the requirements for the role. Since I had been operating in this job voluntarily, I decided to apply for the role when it was finally advertised. Guess what? I didn't get the role. The post was advertised again, I applied a second time, but I still didn't get the position. Later I discovered that this position was awarded to someone who had just completed his Leaving Certificate. I was disheartened and I felt really used. That person had just completed his Leaving Certificate – equivalent to a level 5 in Ireland while my PhD is equivalent to a level 10. He got that role which I had applied for, a role that I was very good at and was training and onboarding other staff. Now, would you say that I had equity or equality? Going forward down the years, this person will go on to have a bachelor's degree in science, apply for a job and will get a much better position than I have, because his CV will show that he has years of work experience. I didn't have the opportunity to get that position – would you call this equity? No, equity doesn't play well for the Black Irish woman, it hasn't worked for me. I can boldly say this is not just a one-off case. This has been happening ever since I started working in the labour market. So, equity doesn't work for the Black Irish woman in my opinion.

9.2 The problem with Black Irish women accessing equity is systemic

When I first arrived in Ireland, I used to think that inequity was related to Black migrants having foreign degree certificates. My first degree was from Nigeria. A certificate from Nigeria is not often given much value in Ireland. For example, a graduate with a medical degree on arrival in Ireland is first told that their qualification is not enough and that they must take a series of exams and pass all of them to be allowed to practise in Ireland. Now that on its own is challenging because after spending 6 years obtaining a university degree, you come to Ireland, and you must write these exams which are quite expensive. Sometimes people have to take these exams 3 or 4 times before they can qualify. I arrived Ireland with a medical degree. I then decided to study for a higher degree instead of taking the exams. I love to teach; I love research work, and I went into further studies to equip myself for the teaching profession and research work. I then obtained more academic qualifications with high hopes of growing in academia. Now it didn't work out as I had planned. The outcome was poor. The system does not provide for equity for Black Irish women. If you look at the workforce in education, you can count on one hand the people of my colour in academia in permanent roles. Some students have never been taught by a Black teacher/lecturer. This does not mean we do not have people fully qualified to lecture in various fields. With medical practitioners like me who want to teach, we are confronted with situations where we are not given the platform to practice our profession and/or to teach. So, the problem is with the system, including the HR (who can be gatekeepers) and recruiters. The Irish system must go back to the drawing board and seek ways to recruit in a way that is equitable. At the same time, it is not about tokenistic equity, diversity, of having 'the' one Black person on the company's team. We need to have an inclusive system. That is where the problem lies. We do not have an inclusive system where we can bring people of colour, Black men and women, people who look like myself into academia. It is beyond performative allyship but walking the talk. Once we can have inclusiveness and take the right action, we won't have any problem with equity and there will be many people like me in academia.

9.3 We need active allies who choose to speak up

A lot can be done for Black Irish women to have equity. We need to bring in legislation that promotes equity for ethnic minorities. This means having a seat at the table and not as an afterthought or add-on to make the event and organisation look good. We want our White friends, White colleagues and White managers to acknowledge our presence. We want them to partner with us. We want them to show human feeling to acknowledge what is not right and consider how they can help in giving Black Irish women a level playing field to thrive. In essence, we want allies. We want to see people of colour when an organisation is talking about inclusiveness not just one person syndrome or a tick box exercise. People of ethnic minorities are better equipped to do certain jobs. Many of us are capable and resilient, and that's a positive for organisations where we are given the opportunity to work. We have to see the Black Irish woman as someone who can do the job, and not just to be used for voluntary, unpaid work. Many Black Irish women are working as volunteers in positions where they are fully qualified to be permanent employees. I remember when I first came to Ireland, I was told that I needed to do a lot of voluntary work so I can put that in my CV, but as I see it now, it did not help in the long run for me, although it might have made a difference for others. As Black Irish women, a lot of our voluntary work is not seen as work experience. People often ask what they can do and how they can help. One simple way is to speak up when we see injustice, inequity, or when people from minority ethnic backgrounds are being unfairly passed over. That's how you can be an active ally. Join us in this campaign. Speak up!

9.4 Most African Irish women do extra work in society in addition to their paid work

I am one of those Black Irish women who has done a lot of voluntary jobs. I'm an activist especially for the younger generation because I am a parent to four sons. When I look at the Ireland of today, I want the Ireland of tomorrow to be better for my children. It is one of my main drivers for volunteering. I am an activist for Black lives. It is my way of saying, *We matter!* People are saying, Black Lives Matter. But I ask, by how much do Black Lives Matter? If our lives matter, it should translate into every area of life and be visible. The society has failed the Black Irish women. We often need to shout for our voices to be heard. Who or what group is actually advocating for us? I mentor young Black children because I want them to grow and learn that there are people of their colour who are doing great things. They have been taught wrongly about their heritage and I want to change that narrative.

We continue to do these voluntary jobs because we want to gain access to the system. Black Irish women do not have many opportunities to showcase themselves. These voluntary roles we take on and create are often used as platforms, or avenues to climb up the ladder in society, to find a voice or visibility for our skills and competencies and to address gaps we see in society affecting our community. So, many Black Irish women who do these voluntary jobs want to get into roles where they can access decision-making levels because we want our voices to matter. We want people to see us for who we are, amazing, beautiful inside out and very hardworking. A few of my friends were having a discussion days ago about how much Black Irish women put into their jobs. You would notice she rarely calls in sick unless she's extremely sick or literally dying! Black Irish women are hardworking, and we want this to be acknowledged and rewarded.

9.5   Meet Dr. Dr. Loveth Owhor – The double Doctor

I have been on a long journey with some highs and lows! I am a qualified medical researcher and I also have a PhD in reproductive medicine. Did I start in the position where I am today? No! I am happy in the role that I am in today,

but this is not the grade I ought to be at now. I started from a very low strata in the world of work. I first came to Ireland as an international student to study for a master's degree. Upon completion, I sought jobs that matched my qualifications, all to no avail. I finally got a job equivalent to someone who has just completed a FETAC level 5 (note my doctorate degree is categorised at level 10 in the Irish education system). I had to down skill to take the FETAC Level 5 training to get the job pitched at that level as I was not getting a job at my highest academic level. How sad do you think that made me! I came to Ireland and completed a master's degree but to get a paid employment, I needed to have an Irish certificate, so I went to do a FETAC level 5 in community care. Not by choice but by necessity. Now, for someone with a master's degree downgraded to that level, you can imagine what it cost me to work my way up the economic ladder (see Joseph 2020). The journey has indeed not been very smooth. It's been a journey of sad and hurtful days. Some days I go back home, and I cry asking myself why I left my birth country. On other days, I come back and I'm like oh yes thank God I am here in Ireland. So, I have mixed emotions. Whenever I am talking about it, I get emotional. It has not been a beautiful journey all the way through. Dr Ebun Joseph has written about the way many Black people in Ireland start at five academic levels lower than their highest academic achievement and sometimes, I say that's my story! (Joseph, 2020; 2022). I am grateful to have come to know other women who share the same struggle as myself. When we come together, we tell our stories and encourage each other. We have a support system which has kept me going. The support system is a bond that has held us together. When we talk about our struggles and our challenges, we also talk about our wins and where we want to go next. So that has been the story from a low level, but I keep going and aiming high, that is what I say to myself, the sky is only the starting point.

References

Joseph, E. 2022. The Wages and Price of Whiteness. Radical History Review. Duke University Press, vol: 2022 (143), p: 79—88.
https://doi.org/10.1215%2F01636545-9593472}.

Joseph, E. 2020. Critical race theory and inequality in the labour market: *Racial stratification in Ireland.*
https://manchesteruniversitypress.co.uk/9781526134394/

10

Equitable work environments should remove barriers

Grace Oladipo
Desk Officer, Department of Foreign Affairs

10.1 Introduction

Equity means creating the conditions, or the environment, that create a level playing field for everyone. It means no one is left behind professionally, developmentally, culturally, socially, intellectually, and mentally. It ensures that regardless of race, gender, or background, they are afforded equal access to opportunities, progression, and success.

One of the best ways to describe equity is using this analogy. Imagine three children trying to watch a football match on the other side of a fence. Child A is 6 metres tall, child B is 5 metres tall, and Child C is 4 metres tall. The fence is 5 metres tall. Child A can see the match perfectly and enjoys the view. Child B was given a step that is 1 metre in height. Child C was given a step that is 2 metres in height. Both Child B and Child C can enjoy the match with the same viewing quality as Child A. That is equity; not giving them all the same opportunity by bringing them to the fence but creating an environment that ensures they are not hindered in experiencing the match by removing their specific barriers, allowing for equal experiences.

10.2 Why Black Irish women do not have equity in the workplace

Black Irish women do not have equity in the labour market in Ireland for various reasons. I wish to highlight three reasons in this chapter: qualifications, connections, and discrimination, bias, and stereotypes.

Qualifications
Regardless of how good an individual's qualification is, if obtained in an African country, it can be challenging to be recognized in Ireland unless you're

a critical skills worker, like a nurse. This means that young African professionals who come to Ireland with prior qualifications must often start from scratch, regardless of their previous work experiences and proven job ability. This impedes their ability to penetrate the labour market on a level that matches their skill set. Instead, they are forced to take lower-paying jobs or return to the educational system, sometimes to get an accreditation they previously had.

Social capital, networks and connections

While studying for my law degree at UCD, I realised I needed to catch up in the first year of my class. Many of my classmates boasted of having parents, family members, and family friends in the legal field. They often reminded me that they didn't have to apply for internships because their parents worked in a firm or knew someone who could help them secure an internship. I didn't know anyone within the legal field in Ireland. At the time, I hadn't met any Black lawyers and was discouraged from pursuing it as a profession. I didn't know anyone who could be an example for me or even have a look at my application apart from the UCD Career Service clinic, who were very helpful and for which I am grateful. I struggled throughout my degree to obtain a legal internship.

The lack of connections meant that as a Black Irish woman looking for the opportunity to establish herself in the legal profession, I was already behind many of my classmates before I started. Although I played my part by networking, reaching out to people on LinkedIn, and working hard, it was clear from the beginning that the playing field needed to be levelled for me to have any equity. This is described as racial stratification where we don't all start at the same point or level (Joseph, 2020).

Discrimination, bias & stereotypes

It is not news that Black women suffer from discrimination and bias in the labour market. A friend of mine experimented and applied for the same job with an identical CV but with two different names, one African and the other Irish. The individual was invited for an interview under the Irish name but not the African name. While we know this happens, it was genuinely shocking to see this play out.

I have been in work spaces where jokes were made about Nigerians, and I was the only Black person in the department. Sometimes, the jokes are subtle, sometimes, they are obvious, but they all point to the same narrative – Black Africans are inferior to White people and cannot work diligently and with integrity. This narrative can drive hiring managers to favour a non-African over a person of African descent regardless of their qualifications and experience.

10.3 We cannot afford to take the easy or quick road regarding equity

Representation is the main problem with Black and African Irish women accessing equity. As someone who was pursuing a legal career, the road less travelled for many Black Irish women, I would often end up in rooms where I was the only Black person. This would mean that I was in a space where I was the minority, and therefore, my ability to contribute value to the room was sometimes overlooked. I am often shocked that hiring managers would say that they do not know how to hire or attract diverse talent, and when given suggestions, they would not implement them. They would have one reason or another as to why those suggestions would not be possible.

See one, be one. In the early part of my studies, it was tough for me to accept that many of the lawyers I looked up to in Ireland did not look like me and that many of the lawyers who did look like me lived in another country. It's often the case that we hear of young African Irish women leaving Ireland to progress in their careers. Part of this is due to a need for more representation. When you cannot see one that looks like you, it almost feels like it will be impossible to attain. When you have fought your whole life, dotted your Is, crossed your Ts, and are still facing barriers in a profession you love, it can push you to look for opportunities outside of Ireland.

Additionally, representation at decision-making levels needs to be improved in Ireland for Black Irish women. Whether governmentally or institutionally, the decision-makers are often White Irish people who may not understand the struggles of Black Irish women in the labour market and have not invited them to give their opinions at the table. When the issues are not discussed or acknowledged, the policies created will not be relevant. Creating policies and rules may be quicker or easier when the affected people are not called to speak at the table. However, the effectiveness of those policies is significantly diminished when it comes to implementation. We cannot afford to take the easy or quick road regarding equity.

Moreover, empathy is easier when we have conversations. Underrepresentation in leadership positions across various industries has impeded the ability of Black Irish women to progress, or progress at a reasonable speed in the labour market. Furthermore, in spaces where Black Irish women are the minority, such as in my profession, the rules are made based on the majority. Therefore, the minority is often forgotten in these spaces and automatically negatively impacted. For example, the idea of a professional hairdo usually comes up in work spaces. By its texture and style, African hair of Black women may not always look like the conventional professional look. When images of a corporate look are shown, they often do not represent what a corporate African woman would look like with natural hair. This is an example of the biases that come into play. Therefore, underrepresentation is one of the biggest reasons for inequity for young Black Irish women in Ireland.

10.4 Interrogate your DEI strategy, its effectiveness and its WHY.

Unfortunately, many diversity, equity, and inclusion (DEI) programmes have proven to be more performative than action based. Usually, companies, industries, and institutions will implement a 'strategy' or plan to attract more diverse talent to create a level playing field. However, deeply rooted in the foundation of many of these plans is a sense that 'we'll keep doing what we're doing', 'we'll be happy if we attract one, or it should be written down even if it doesn't make a difference'.

My challenge to institutions as they read this is to consider these four questions:

1. Why are you creating a DEI strategy? Is it because you 'have to' based on trends or because you genuinely believe in the power of diversity and equity?
2. Who is writing your DEI strategy? Is it written by a group of people who look like and represent the version of Ireland that we live in today or a group of people from the same background?

3. Whose voices are loudest? Is it the voices of those who have always had access to the labour market or those who have been impeded by multiple barriers and still managed to overcome them?
4. What does your DEI strategy consist of? Is it based only on plans to make the work environment conducive for people from minority backgrounds, or does it include plans to equip unemployed people from minority backgrounds with the tools they might need to access your roles?

The truth is that the performative commitments to equity have become extraordinarily tiring, and it has become relatively easy to see through them. Additionally, more education is required. Leaders, decision-makers, and employees must be educated across industries about their biases, stereotypes, and the subtle discrimination that can occur. I thoroughly appreciate work spaces that make DEI training mandatory for employees. I also appreciate work spaces that create a healthy and comfortable culture for individuals to report discriminatory or biased conduct. Nevertheless, we must go beyond a one-off training. After the online training, a mandatory roundtable discussion with colleagues from diverse backgrounds should follow where experiences are shared. This real-time, real-life dialogue tells employees the need to address biases is close to home. Hearing their colleagues explain how even the subtlest of jokes can make them feel bad, will make them more aware and curious to receive more information. Online training is excellent, but sometimes, it makes it easy to forget the human behind the diversity training.

Finally, there is a need to create more programmes to integrate Black and African Irish women into working spaces. I equip young women with the tools they need to access the labour market and global opportunities. I realised that there is often a gap between qualified young people and their desired careers. This gap is usually because they may have difficulty conveying their qualifications and skills in written applications or interviews. Because of the need for more representation, it is often complicated for these women to reach out to someone within their desired profession who could point them in the right direction where their applications are concerned. *That is where the bridge is needed.* By creating programmes that give insight into an institution or company (which is what most institutions do), and by providing tools to people from minority backgrounds to access their labour market, equity is getting closer. More programmes are needed to give Black Irish women access to the labour market and help them integrate into it.

10.5 Most Black Irish women do extra work in society besides paid work

I think most Black Irish women do extra work in society in addition to their paid work because of pay disparities with their White Irish counterparts. They often have to do these voluntary roles to get other experiences in the hope that it might help them get higher roles. Additionally, as I said earlier, they are often unable to use their academic qualifications when they come to Ireland, requiring them to either take up another qualification or work in low-paying jobs to make ends meet. This did not apply to me as I studied in Ireland, which has notably reduced my barriers to high-paying jobs. However, some of my Black Irish colleagues who despite getting their qualifications in Ireland have still been unable to secure a high-paying job due to various barriers and have had to take on additional jobs to get by.

10.5 Meet Grace Oladipo: How systemic barriers *almost* changed my professional course

I am deeply thankful for my journey to my current role. Although I faced barriers, I also encountered incredible people along the way who were willing to take a chance on me, invest in me, and push me toward my goals. I am

deeply grateful to every single teacher, professor, and mentor who called out the greatness inside me and created the environment that would nurture it and make me the person I am today.

My family migrated to Ireland when I was eight years old, and I grew up within the Irish educational system and I got to study the Irish language. This reduced a lot of barriers, as I understood the educational system and grew up within Irish society. Throughout primary and secondary school, I had teachers who ensured I was not disadvantaged based on my background and showed me how to play to my strengths.

I completed a BCL at UCD and throughout my time there, I participated in various extra-curricular activities. I worked part-time at various places throughout my degree, including Nando's Liffey Valley, and on UCD campus. When I struggled with my studies I turned to extra-curricular fun with singing, dancing, and acting to get me through. I played to my strengths, despite the barriers I faced. This approach helped me to excel academically and socially, and I was awarded the UCD President's Award and the Arthur Cox Contribution to University Life Award. I was interested in social enterprise and I started a few organisations aimed at improving the quality of life of marginalised people.

I was not successful in getting a legal internship during my degree, but I received an accounting internship at PwC instead. I am deeply grateful for the accounting internship, but this is another story of how our life course as Black Irish women can be easily reprogrammed. Why could I not get a legal internship? As there are very few legal practitioners of African descent in Ireland surely some of the law firms might have been keen to provide an internship to a qualified person of African descent?

Nevertheless, my accounting internship was my first step into the corporate world, and this opened up many opportunities for me. I started my tax training contract with PwC after completing my degree but after a short while, I realised that my true professional passion was in law, and I became even more determined to overcome the barriers I had earlier faced. I moved from PwC to study for a master's degree in international human rights law at the University of Notre Dame, Indiana, US on a Fulbright and George Moore scholarship. The experience will forever be one of the highlights of my career, as it cemented my desire to be a human rights educator.

After my master's degree, I received sponsorship to study at The Hague Academy of International Law in the Netherlands. There I had the opportunity to work with renowned human rights lawyers and meet judges of the International Court of Justice. Shortly afterwards, I was selected to work at the Office of the United Nations High Commissioner for Human Rights in Geneva. Working first-hand on human rights policies and attending UN Sessions at the Palais des Nations was really a life-changing experience. I currently work as a Desk Officer in the Department of Foreign Affairs in Dublin. Outside of my day job, I contribute to the community where I work to equip women from minority ethnic backgrounds with the tools that they need to overcome the barriers that they face in the labour market.

11
Black Irish women and equity in the workplace

Ellie Kisyombe
Founder, 'Ellie's Kitchen Home Edition', political aspirant, activist

11.1 Introduction

I'll start by saying that I am a Black Irish woman who has done a lot and strives every day to set up companies and to be in a position whereby I could be valuable to the nation. I don't see Black Irish women having equity at all. We are very, very far from it. There is a general lack of trust in the capacity of Black women to deliver results, even though the evidence shows that we deliver every day. Due to stigma and stereotypes, Black Irish women are often undermined and denied opportunities in the labour market, which makes it very hard for us. I would say that we are very far from achieving equity in the labour market in general.

11.2 The problem with Black Irish women accessing equity

The main issue of concern is the lack of trust in Black Irish women. I have come to realise that there is a persistent lack of information on potential economic opportunities, building structures, funding, and grants. It is always a challenge for an individual like me to access and be granted these facilities equitably. There are too many barriers in our way. There are more hoops for us to jump through. So, we as Black Irish woman usually have to work extra hard to get the same result as others.

11.3 What do we need for Black women to have equity?

Working out what is needed for Black Irish women to have equity in Ireland is a difficult question to answer. But I believe the solution is basically the elimination of barriers. For example, one of the barriers to accessing equity is a change in perception. If people of White Irish descent could recognize the value brought into the community by people who look like me and if everyone could try to be less fearful, and work together, I believe we could really make a difference. Any initiative that would foster mutual learning and understanding between established and newer communities/arrivals would really be of benefit.

The fear of being overshadowed can stifle cooperation and hinder the opportunities to get together. But if we view each other as partners in a venture, supporting and allowing representation at the table, transformative change is possible. The key, in my view, lies in acknowledging the power dynamics, embracing change, and creating space for every person to contribute positively.

11.4 Most Black Irish women are resilient

There's inherent self-resilience and power within Black Irish women. We are often underestimated, but we are catalysts for change. We have demonstrated the ability to make a difference, with or without financial resources or compensation, and sometimes without acknowledgement. We are capable mothers and wonderful home makers. We are adaptable and good at managing financial challenges, we navigate the monthly salary cycle, ensuring our children are fed. Our unique energy, which is rooted in our cultural upbringing can be intimidating to others. However, if we recognize this power as a tool that is beneficial to society, it will be a win, win for everyone.

> *Black Irish women are often underestimated, but*
> *we are catalysts for change.*

The Black community in Ireland should strive to collaborate, leveraging our collective accomplishments. The Black and African community in Ireland must acknowledge the strength in our unity; as the saying goes, "When there is one, there is nothing; when there are two or three, there is power." Black individuals should harness this power to build a collective future. I believe that in 5 years from now, if we work together, we could establish a robust equity, which would lead to the emergence of many new business ventures which are initiated and led by Black Irish women.

11.5 Ellie Kisiyombe's journey in Ireland

I am a co-founder of Our Table, Dublin and the founder of 'Ellie's Kitchen Home Edition'. I am a mother, a political aspirant and an activist. I moved to Ireland over 10 years ago. I found myself in the Direct Provision system, where I became an advocate, campaigning to end the system and change aspects that were dehumanising both to the adults in the system and the young people

who are often in and out of school, embarrassed as their schoolmates know they are in the hostel system or just from being moved from one city to the other without much notice and having to start a new school and make new friends. Through our collective efforts, we successfully lobbied the government for change, and while it is not yet perfect, people in the asylum system now have a better life with room for continuous change till the system is brought to an end. As a woman actively working to transform the system, in 2019, I ran for political office as a counsellor. Although I didn't secure the position, it was a significant campaign which had an impact in Ireland. Since then, I have collaborated with various boards, and currently, I have established my company, Ellie's Kitchen Home Edition. I supply food condiments to major supermarkets and I employ over 30 people. So, yeah, it's been quite a journey, and I'm proud of the progress I've made.

12

Women of African descent face racial and gender bias at work

Sola Mobolaji
Senior Social Worker

12.1 Introduction

Women of African descent face bias at work. Although all women groups experience bias at work, Black and African Irish women face racial and gender bias at work. For all women who are working, there are stereotypes, pay inequality and we are the ones that, for one reason or another, are responsible for taking care of the home and the children. This extra caregiving role comes with an extra burden of time and availability and biases the workplace experiences of women that somehow, they cannot deliver in the labour market like the men can. For Black and African Irish women, the intersectionality of gender and race exacerbates the issue further, making it even more difficult for them to enjoy equality in society or to experience equity at work.

There is basically little to no representation from women of African descent in leadership roles in Ireland. In areas of skills shortage, especially in the lower skilled sectors (e.g. carers) there are high numbers of Black women in that area of work. These are "areas of least resistance" (Joseph, 2020). And many Black Irish women do not take up these jobs by choice but simply because of economic necessity. In all sectors very few Black Irish women occupy management roles, despite their high numbers at the entry levels. In my profession I do meet other Black Irish social workers. But as the pyramid goes higher, it becomes Whiter and Whiter.

From my personal experience and observation, I have seen on two different occasions, colleagues whose skills and performance in the job I had consistently outperformed over the years being offered leadership training, while I was left out. I had to face the sad fact that if I was White, I would have progressed faster in my career. In fact, I was also around to witness the struggles of these colleagues when they were placed in the new positions which they couldn't handle.

I thought if I had been given that same opportunity, support and coaching, I would definitely have done better. I say that because in the community, and in other areas where I actually led different projects, I was able to deliver and do well.

12.2 Ireland is still lacking representation of minority groups in the labour market

The lack of representation at management levels in Ireland is a major problem and a big part of why we don't have equity for Black Irish women. In other countries, there are many Black women who have progressed in their careers. Some of the barriers have been broken down and it's wonderful to see more individuals of African descent leading in their respective fields. Representation really helps and encourages others coming behind. In Ireland, we are lagging behind when it comes to representation of all groups in the labour market.

Stereotypes

There are a lot of stereotypes attached to people of African descent in Ireland. Although we are strong and assertive women, we are often mislabelled as aggressive or confrontational. You often hear stories like, 'they can't do it', 'they are not competent', 'they can't speak good English', these are some of the typical stereotypes held about Black people in Ireland. I sometimes wonder about this because for most people of African descent, while English is not their first language, education in a country like Nigeria is in English. And many Black Irish women have bachelors and master's degrees, with some holding 2 master's degrees and or PhD. Yet, they still have to face this stereotype...it doesn't seem fair.

Limited access to resources

Black and African Irish women don't have the same opportunities, support, or network as their White peers in the labour market even when they have the same or sometimes higher qualifications. The network is also a key resource which unfortunately, this group lacks. There is an existing/organic network that easily connects people in Ireland. I always say people are cousins to each other. We see that there is always somebody that knows somebody, that knows somebody. People of African descent have not been able to build that network yet. This is not because they do not have the ability but the time (in years) it takes to build these networks. For example, many women of African descent did not complete their primary and secondary education in Ireland. Neither are their extended family members in Ireland.

So, a really important question is "who do you know?" Sometimes, in the labour market, especially in leadership roles, who you know really matters. Someone who can actually mention your name and say, "Oh, I actually worked with this person. This person is good and able to deliver," that kind of informal recommendation makes a huge difference and really helps people to progress. Joseph (2021) discusses how social capital is a resource but it's one that is used by our White counterparts. As valuable as this resource is, we cannot monitor it, add it as credit, mention it, or legislate against it.

12.3 Support Black African Irish women to get leadership positions

For Black African Irish women to have equity in the labour market, those barriers that I mentioned earlier need to go. There's the need for representation, there's the need for more opportunities for Black Irish women. Organisations should assess the level of real representation and diversity in their leadership. Support Black Irish women to build up their skill set and reach the leadership positions they want, by coaching and mentoring them properly, giving them management training and opportunities to deputise in roles. They also have to be included and invited to be part of the network. A fair system in place where everyone will have equal opportunities and access to progress in our chosen field is what we would strive for.

12.4 Most Black Irish women are doing too much in addition to paid work

Black Irish women are a minority, we are the homemakers and many of us are the sole providers for our families. We often have to work and take care of our children at the same time. Some also are providers to their extended families. All of this pressure means that many Black Irish women take extra jobs and do extra degrees and more education in the hope of getting a management job or building up their careers.

Many African Irish women are not entitled to any kind of funding. They are working full time, so they have no study grants. In addition, many return to college. This puts extra pressure on their finances as they have to pay the fees. Think about it, how do they cope financially? Most of them have to get a second job. Unfortunately, I have seen Black African Irish women collapse when they're trying to complete a master's degree, work full-time and look after a family of up to four children. There are many Black Irish women with health issues dealing with high blood pressure, and other stress-related health issues simply because they are doing too much.

I have been in that situation myself. I used to work at two jobs. But I have a very good friend, who was the one who actually made me think. She told me, *"No, what you have is what you're going to spend. The more you earn, the more you're going to spend anyway. So, you have to just stay within your means and mind yourself. You need to mind your mental health, mind your physical health."* She was the one who really made me stop working at the second job. And I'm grateful for that good advice. Many of us just do too much. Our extended family are outside Europe and cannot easily come to Ireland like other European country migrants can. We feel responsible for the relatives back home, we want to break down barriers and we are ambitious, we want to build our career. So, we put a lot of pressure on ourselves.

12.5 Meet Sola Mobolaji - Coaching makes a difference in the workplace

When I came to Ireland nearly 25 years ago, I came with a postgraduate degree. However, when I first starting working, I was not using my postgraduate degree. It was so difficult in the late 1990s and early 2000s. I remember registering my certificates and trying to seek employment, and someone told me, "*Oh, your certificates are not recognized.*" I was a bit shocked as I knew my degree from the University of Lagos, one of the very good universities, actually is recognized in most Western countries. However, employers and recruiters in Ireland were not informed. I decided to return to college for another postgraduate degree to increase my value. I realised I was not going to stay in that role because at the time I was working as a social care worker, and the work hours were very long. At the time, my children were very young. I think I worked in the role for a couple of months, then I requested for my transcripts, and I decided to return to school and obtain qualification as a social worker. I had to complete a postgraduate degree in social policy and then in social work.

After my training, I now have three postgraduate degrees, because getting a permanent job was not easy at that time, unlike now, when Ireland is desperately in need of social workers. The system in place then was that the jobs were there but were usually short-term contracts for people of colour, until the government started a national panel programme (where everyone is assessed based on their performance). In my opinion, it reduced bias. It helped many people of colour and migrants because many of us that were professional, were able to get on to this panel.

For example, if you come in at number 5 or number 10 on the panel, well you know, definitely you will get the job. That was how many of us got permanent roles then. From then on, as I mentioned earlier, some people had managers who took them under their wings and mentored them. One of my friends was so desperate to progress in her career that she eventually relocated to the UK. She has been very successful in her career in the UK.

We only have two principal social workers who are Black Irish women at the moment in Ireland. This person I refer to has gone further than that, in a very short space of time. For me, the journey can be really draining when you don't have mentorship, coaching, when you don't have that support base, and you see others just getting it. Networking comes automatically to them. Friendship comes automatically to them. They are not faced with the racial barriers, the discrimination, the lack of representation; there is nobody putting you forward and you know your capacity, you know how you function well in other areas.

I am in my 50s, and even before I came to Ireland, I had career progression and I know where I was and I know where my colleagues are now. It can be challenging when you being pushed to prove yourself again and again. Don't forget that we don't have the support of our extended family and we really miss that. We also need to invest more time to our children to give them a good start so that they don't have to go through what we went through, whether in the labour market or on the street.

I am thankful for the opportunities I have now. I am forever grateful to the person I call my mentor. He somehow just believes in me. If there is any job opportunity on offer, he will let me know, and then I will apply for it. He would say *"Shola, you are good. I'm sure you're going to be very good at this. Go and do this. Go and put in for this."* So, I have a career path now. I can say he doesn't know what he has done really, but by just giving me those opportunities that I wouldn't have known existed, he has helped me so much.

So, mentors who know us and have worked with us for a long time are so valuable. They encourage us and bring us to those places where we can actually move and progress in our career and even identify the qualities or skill set that we didn't know we had.

I have faced those barriers. Yes, I have experienced them, and unfortunately, I am still experiencing them. However, there's light because I have people who believe in me. I have one or two people who believe in supporting my career and they are helping me to progress in the areas I want to develop in. If people can be more open and can help us women and not judge us, pull us down or discriminate against us, if they tried to spend a bit of time to understand who we are and how capable we are, I believe that would make a huge difference.

13

A double disadvantage not just as women, but as Black women

Eya Lawani
SNA and Social Justice Advocate

13:1 Introduction

As a first generation Black Irish woman, an equitable labour market would be one which recognizes difference or diversity by providing tailored and specific supports to mediate racial difficulties. It recognizes that although women as a group have been traditionally and historically sidelined in labour markets because of gender biases, Black Irish women as a sub-group within the wider women's group, face other difficulties such as racial biases as well, which might not impact their peers who do not have a Black identity. The concept of equity is different from that of equality in its broader usage. From my personal experience, Black Irish women do not have an equitable outcome in the Irish labour market, although I am aware that Ireland is striving to create equality for all. While equality focuses on creating 'sameness' or treating all women as 'equals', equity is more nuanced, recognising that the bare conditions of people's lives are different and therefore unique challenges intersect to create inequality for some more than others.

In this context an example is racism against Black people as a group, which may require unique considerations by employers in order to allow for equity. Equality operates on the basis that giving 'equal access or opportunity' to all women as a group will help the majority of women gain parity. Equity on the other hand, recognizes and insists that this may not be enough to level the playing field for Black women within the larger group of women. For the Black Irish woman to experience equity in the Irish labour market, the system has to take cognizance of specific barriers which impact Black women disproportionately compared to White women. I specifically refer to racism here as it can still impact how Black women function in workplaces, *even when equal access has been granted*.

Black Irish women will initially require tailored supports that acknowledges our specific vulnerabilities, not just as women, but as that intersectional identity tagged "the Black woman", recognizing that in some contexts, we might need different supports, without framing this as a weakness. So, while an equality focused labour market might recognize and try to mediate the commonly acknowledged barriers which impact all women accessing work, like negative patriarchal societal attitudes, legislation around maternity cover, provision of childcare facilities, and flexible work hours for those with young families, an equitable workplace would need to consider other additional factors specifically targeted at Black Irish women.

An obvious support could be the provision of education around racism, the examination of historical systemic and institutional practices which exclude 'ethnic people' and attitudes which create difficult work dynamics for minorities. These situations often leave Black Irish women feeling isolated and unsupported in the workplace, and impacting their performances or making their jobs stressful and unsustainable. Looking through a racial lens and my lived experiences as a first generation Black Irish woman with migrant origins, I cannot say that the Irish labour market has been set up to give Black women equity. Even as a naturalized Irish citizen, I still encounter difficulty being acknowledged and treated as an equal with people who do not have a Black Identity.

Some of the barriers to equitable treatment in the workplace are generally gendered and therefore faced by all women as a group, there are racial dimensions, which intersect to create specific challenges that are unique and exclusive to Black women. This can be seen where there are exclusions on the basis of 'foreign sounding names' or being commonly stereotyped as 'angry and difficult to work with in teams'. These narratives can unconsciously bias employers even before Black women have been given the opportunity to present themselves at interview. It is common knowledge that women as a group already struggle with unequal access to certain types of employment or work spaces.

This kind of inequity is not about capability or an absence of the skill set required to do a job, it is about socially constructed conditions such as unconscious biases about the place of women in society. This condition is further amplified for Black Irish women who are a minority within a minority in Irish society. Seeing Black women as part of the formal workforce is certainly not commonplace and is a relatively new phenomenon in Ireland, but what is undeniable is that the combination of race and gender creates a double bind for those Black women who are trying to access and grow in the world of work.

If we consider that historically the Irish labour market has mainly been male-dominated except for particular workspaces which are traditionally viewed as 'women's work', such as primary school teaching and nursing, then the double intersection of race and gender means that Black Irish women, who are sparsely represented in the Irish labour market anyway, risk facing the same confining attitudes which seek to limit them to certain areas of work like carers or low-paid jobs in the informal job sector, thus recreating not just gender restrictions but racial ones too. Having acknowledged this inequity and recognising that racial bias is an additional dimension of discrimination or inequity, it is obvious that Black women face a double disadvantage not just as women, but as Black women.

13.2. Systemic barriers hinder Black Irish women from accessing equity

A mix of social, cultural and systemic factors together often result in barriers which disproportionately impact, exclude, and disadvantage women who identify as Black Irish. Socially, a lack of understanding of diversity can result in conflicts because of insensitivity or disrespect of difference. This can result in workplace practices, which though considered the norm for the hegemonic majority, might actually be insensitive to the needs of the few who might become labelled as the problem, or seen as socially incompatible with certain spaces. An example is Black women being expected to modify their appearance to fit into 'western dress codes', and who are made to feel inadequate or uncomfortable when they wear their ethnic or traditional clothes at work, because it is perceived as 'not professional' in certain spaces.

Culturally, attempts to control women's appearances in the workplace (although subtle), can mean that for Black women, issues around their hair or afro or hair styles they might choose to wear can actually affect their job! It is no exaggeration to say that hair can limit their access to certain spaces or positions, effectively locking her out of certain sectors of the labour market and/or limiting her progress if employers see their 'image' as problematic. Even when access is granted, systemic and institutional biases can often mean that performances of 'diversity' masking as 'inclusion' could become used as tools to signal compliance with integration requirements, without actually respecting people as equals. Sometimes individuals are used as tokens to create distortion in the field, making equity or fairness difficult to achieve.

Moreover, the social capital and network needed to access certain work spaces can almost be non-existent for Black Irish women as a minority group in Ireland.

Also, recognition and representation in some organisational hierarchies show that progression beyond certain levels is problematic, not because Black Irish women do not have the skills or qualifications, but because as first generation citizens, Black Irish women are still relative newcomers to the Irish workforce and have only become visible in the last maybe 25 years or less. So even where gender parity considerations are applied, the Irish woman still has an advantage over their Black or African origin peer, even when their qualifications and skills are the same.

13.3. Affirmative action can make the labour market more equitable

Some of the unique challenges facing Black Irish women as they try to access the Irish labour market includes the absence of extended families or originating nurturing communities where they grew up and felt safe. While many women might take that family support base and the range of services it provides for granted, like childcare in the case of women with young families, its absence is a significant barrier to working outside the home for those who do not have it. For Black Irish women who might be first generation Irish, they might still be grappling with social and cultural differences, making work dynamics tricky.

This can be difficult to manage in organisations which do not recognize that just having a diverse workforce alone does not necessarily make the organisation an inclusive workplace. For those who come from a culture which still traditionally positions women as homemakers, it can be difficult to transition to working outside the home. This can result in terminations or suspensions where employers are unwilling or unable to allow for any flexibility around these unique challenges.

A positive work culture that supports everybody equally allows all workers to flourish, but equity demands that the labour market recognize that a continuum of support is needed for those who while also benefiting from the general supports in place, will need targeted and tailored interventions when particular concerns which do not impact others in the same way are identified or flagged. An example might be the use of affirmative action as one of the tools for creating access and spaces for women as a group to be represented in the workplace. This same concept can be applied within the group to ensure that Black women who happen to be in the minority and sometimes face specific discriminations that other non-Black women might not face in their day-to-day interactions, are protected.

Racism needs to be addressed and tackled to protect Black women from the microaggressions which sometimes mask as 'culture' and go unchallenged, especially when certain practices have been normalised in wider society which often tends to disregard issues that affect women as a group. Having policies in place that educate and address racism would mean that workplaces are actively and pro-actively promoting a safe and equitable workplace instead of just being reactionary in protecting their staff who might be impacted by discriminatory practices.

13.4. Going down to go up – my career journey in Ireland

I have personally experienced a lot of dissonance in my journey through the  Irish labour market, and still do. I am conscious that my trajectory is not unique to me but common enough amongst Black migrant women as a community. I arrived in Ireland 24 years ago as a graduate of political science, with 5 years' work experience in Nigeria before emigrating. My desire to contribute to Irish society by joining the labour market here was often met with resistance by employers who seemed to think that foreign degrees equalled inferior education, or that my qualifications were not equivalent to an Irish education or standard. Many, therefore, required that I get some kind of Irish qualification to be able to access the Irish workforce.

While waiting for the verification of my degree certificate from my home country of Nigeria by the National Qualifications Authority in Ireland, I decided to access a level 5 and 6 FETAC training in Childcare and Healthcare support, as up until that time, most of my job applications were unsuccessful on the grounds that I did not have Irish qualifications or experience. I had to down skill as well as go back three steps from my Level 8 qualification to engage with basic training before I could access the Irish labour. This is a systemic and institutional problem which means that skilled and competent workers are often undermined and undervalued because they do not hold Irish certificates, meaning that a lot of Black Irish women are often overlooked or passed over in a country which claims to be looking for qualified skilled workers.

On reflection, the change in my career path was probably due to an awareness that as a Black migrant woman, it seemed to be easier at the time to get care work than any other work, as that seemed to be the space where women like me were more visible and seemingly more accepted. While there is nothing wrong with working as a carer, it was not the career path I had ever envisaged for myself. I started thinking about how representation works in society and how it frames groups. I started thinking how people of African descent have been perceived and how we have been presented in Irish society. I worry that this might have legacy implications which will impact young Black Irish citizens who are beginning to access the labour market.

Following my new interest in the areas of social care and advocacy for children and young people, on completion of the FETAC levels 5 and 6, I started working as a youth worker in a detention school for teenage boys. As one of the only Black women working in that establishment, I was very aware that I was charting a path and serving as a visual representation to others from my community who could then see that it was possible for us to be in other spaces that I had thought were closed to my community. As soon as my degree was verified and accepted by the Qualifications Authority in Ireland, I started studying for a postgraduate diploma in conflict and dispute resolution at TCD. Its focus on mediation and alternative dispute resolution as a tool for dealing with young offenders, while keeping them out of the criminal justice system, aligned with my desire to advocate for best practice when it came to keeping vulnerable young people safe. At this point, it was clear to me as a Black migrant woman and a mother, that our Black Irish children could easily become socially framed as "problematic" due to a lack of understanding of diversity, which was a fairly new trend with the increased rate of immigration into Ireland that was happening at the time. This lack of understanding and support could impair the future chances of accessing the labour market and therefore affect the chances of having equal access to work, disadvantaging the next generation of Black Irish people.

In the hope of tackling some of these concerns, 10 years later, in 2019 with support from University College Dublin Lifelong Learning and a 'Cothrom na Féinne' scholarship programme, which aims to promote justice and equality for women from minority groups, I pursued a master's degree in equality studies, while working full- time in a special school supporting children with intellectual disabilities.

While I am thankful that my journey has been fairly rewarding despite some barriers and obstacles, I am hopeful that my daughter who is second generation, Irish born and a Black woman, will not face the same obstacles of discrimination, lack of respect, unequal access to work, promotion, recognition, and remuneration that I have faced. I am also hopeful that my sons, who are the next generation of young Black Irish men, will be afforded the environment to be fully Irish with equal access to work as their peers, without being systematically disadvantaged and placing unnecessary obstacles in their paths by because of racism as they access the Irish labour market.

14

Black Irish women carry a double burden

Kathleen Lynch
Professor of Equality Studies Emerita, University College Dublin.
Senior Lectureship (Associate Professorship) in Education.
Commissioner with the Irish Human Rights and Equality Commission (IHREC)

14.1 Introduction

I would prefer to talk about equality, as it is more meaningful in policy and legal terms. I suppose to begin, women are the inferior sex. That is where we start for Black Irish women as well. We may not like it, but women are the second sex, as Simone de Beauvoir noted in the 1940s. They are what men are not, and being a man is not to be a woman. While men are generally expected to dominate and control the world including the world of employment, women are not assigned this role. This means that women are implicitly second-class subordinated citizens. From that point of view, the problem for Black women generally, and Black Irish women is that they carry a double burden; they are part of the inferior feminine class but they are also exposed to colour-based racism at the same time.

If the feminine is the inferior category, then there is always an uphill struggle to define the feminist perspective as a way of organising society, as a way of organising work, and as a way of doing things differently. The major institutions of society and work bureaucracies are built around a very particular masculine model of citizenship, a masculinity built on the notion of the dominance of subordinates. Black Irish women, like all women, are subject to this. This is very well documented in the literature (Connell, 1995; Connell & Wood, 2005; Lister 2003).

In most cultures, and in most Western cultures particularly, masculinity is equated with exercising power and control at work, in the family and in political life; femininity is defined much more in terms of service, so girls and women are socialised more into deference and to service. Most women are not socialised into exercising authority and control. They are socialised to be quiet and gentle. They literally learn how to speak quietly; they don't learn how to use their voice. In fact, they often never get their voice. I think these are very fundamental cultural mores (traditions) that affect women generally, including Black Irish women.

Ireland is a Western society and a predominantly White, male-dominated society. White people, including White women, have lived and benefited indirectly or directly from the privilege of Whiteness. We may not see it that way, but of course by virtue of our White skin, White women are always beneficiaries of the racial dividend.

14.2 The Western cultural frame has an inherent assumption of racial superiority

There are very particular equality problems for Black Irish women. The first problem is that most Irish people are White and are not used to seeing Black people as equal to themselves. It is as blunt as that. And the stereotypes that we have inherited, including those from religion, for example, even though it is not intended, the metaphor of Black as a symbol of evil is a very fundamental cultural narrative. The colour Black is equated with the devil, with things that are bad (Tsri, 2015). As metaphors and images are read in cultural and historical context, the normative and moral consequences of categorising Blackness or darkness as a symbol of absence, or even evil, is highly significant. That metaphor of Blackness frames how we relate to people whose colour of skin is not white; it impacts on people, even if they can never name it. You have to struggle against that; we have to educate people out of it, but I think we are a long way from achieving that. We have a very long way to go to see Black people as equal to White people as colour-based racism is endemic to so much Western European thinking.

It seems so amazing in some ways that somebody should even notice the colour of someone's skin. But we learned those racial stereotypes in multiple ways – formally through education and the media, but also in the context of pursuing 'good' intentions. Many Irish people travelled across the world, to 'do good' as they saw it, to spread Christianity. But, of course, they operated within a Western culture frame, with its inherent assumptions of racial superiority. As the history of Africa shows, the colonisers or missionaries frequently didn't respect the culture of the local people in African countries, or their values and their way of life. Many Irish people became part of the colonial class. They returned with this mentality. We had, as you know, the Black babies' boxes (where those who were Black were seen only as an object of charity, poor, and ignorant). We had no understanding of the sophisticated cultures, and the sustainable ways of life operating across so many African countries. We did not know that there was much greater equality between women and men in many of these countries than there was in Ireland. Because we are embedded in White supremacism, which is part of Eurocentrism, we were party to the colonising class, and blind to learning from those who were colonised. We assumed that European traditions and cultures were superior to others. European culture was represented as the pinnacle of 'civilisation'. Nobody mentioned all the wars, nobody mentioned the killing, the brutality that went with European colonisation, be it military, cultural, economic or political. The assumption was 'West was best', that Europeans were 'superior people' and that everybody else should learn from them. The lives of Indigenous peoples were treated cheaply in the interests of colonisation (Patel and Moore, 2018). So, there is a huge unlearning, a decolonisation of our minds that needs to occur. We urgently need to learn African history. We also need to decolonise the curricula in schools and universities; we need to learn how to respect as equals those people who are different from ourselves.

14.3 Opening up to other groups is not a threat, it expands our world

Many people might not know this, but a lot of people who are Black or Brown in Ireland are very highly qualified as their reasons for migrating to Ireland are very different to those who migrated to France or the UK from the former colonies. The issue is not that Black Irish women (or men) lack qualifications, skills or competences; rather they lack opportunities. However, they do have problems getting their qualifications recognized. This is an important message to put out there. I think a lot of Irish people assume automatically, following the racial stereotype, that they have learned from their childhood, that those whose skin is Black could not possibly be as well qualified as they are. That is the first thing that must be challenged as it is untrue.

But I also think we need more pro-active programmes if we are to include Black Irish women in particular, and Black Irish men, in positions of power. I often say in my own head: there will be equality in Ireland when I see a series of people who are Black, especially Black Irish women, in very senior positions running big public sector organisations and big companies, and where that is not called into question, or even noticed. We are a long way from that. We need programmes, active programmes where we set out plans, strategies, training, targets, and timeframes to actually make this happen. It will not happen by accident. It is about having reasonable accommodation not only on disability grounds but on colour, gender, carer, social class, and other grounds.

Having people who are culturally different is very valuable in work organisations, as people can learn from outsiders within; they can learn to see the world from a different angle. Opening up to somebody different is a privilege, an opportunity to expand our world; it is not a threat.

I remember Ebun Joseph telling me, if she doesn't mind me telling this story, about her son and when he earned his first wage in his first paid job. He had to distribute the money here and there to the rest of the family because all his family had contributed and enabled him to get to that place. And I thought, that is so insightful, such a beautiful expression of gratitude. That says so much about the community spirit that you have come from Ebun, but we don't have that culture. The first thing young people do here in Ireland when they get money is they see what they'll spend it on for themselves. I often think we, as Irish people, have so much to learn from African and other cultures, in terms of how they learn from an early age to think of others. We need to learn from people who are unfamiliar to us, and say 'Right, this person has a different cultural background, they have a different set of values, what could I learn from this?' It is not only creating places and spaces and creating programmes of inclusion but also recognising culturally and intellectually what we could learn; it is about owning our own cultural limitations.

For example, we have a very 'I-centred' culture, everything is about the 'I'. This is reflected in the marketing of technology, notably the I-phone. But we know from what is happening with climate change, from war, that we need a more 'We-centred' culture. Not that we shouldn't respect the individual, but we need to think of the community and society and of how we can be creating a sense of belonging for everybody (Lynch 2022). That is something that is much stronger in other countries, especially in a number of sub-Saharan African and South-American countries. We did have a cooperative tradition in Ireland, the 'Meitheal', supporting each other in times of need, especially harvesting crops, working together, building and creating communities, but a lot of that cooperative culture has been lost. We could learn a lot from other cultures about how to re-ignite the Meitheal tradition on a larger scale.

Let's come back to talk about women and employment. Women, generally speaking, often won't even apply for a job until they know they are nearly overqualified for it. This is true. Men will 'throw in a CV', women are far less likely to do this unless they know they 'tick all the boxes.' I think we need to put out recruitment calls, for example, that expressly invite Black Irish women to apply and make it clear they will be welcomed and supported if successful. This is more than just one line in an advertisement. It needs to be made clear that people who have a different skin colour or ethnicity are welcome because of what they would contribute, because they bring extra value to the organisation.

I also think the care role that women play in life has to be considered as well. Women are primary carers, not just of children but of older family members who are dependent e.g., sick or elderly parents etc, they are the ones doing all the social networking work of the household, which is a second job for most women. There must be reasonable accommodation of carers in employment situations. We also urgently need proper publicly funded, accessible and well-resourced childcare. Without it, we absolutely won't have any women of any class, colour, or creed having equal opportunities with men in the labour market.

The rate of maternity and paternity (and paid parental) benefit at €27450 per week is only one third of the gross average weekly earnings in Ireland. This makes taking maternity leave very costly. While unpaid parental leave is allowed, only better-off workers can take this option. The fact that 46% of women on maternity benefit did not receive a top up from their employers (in 2019) shows that many women have to return to work as soon as possible[i]Unless men are incentivised to take on childcare and care of other people on equal terms with the women in their lives, women will never have equality. Doing hands-on care work must become a source of pride and status for men. Now, that may take time, but it will happen eventually, if we work for it.

The figures (from the Central Statistics Office) I was examining recently showed me that the employment rate for men is now approximately 70%; for women it is 59%. Why? Because women have to give up their jobs or go to work part time because of the cost of childcare, which is overwhelmingly run on a commercial basis. This is crazy and highly inefficient. Women are also the people, who do most of the care of older people in their own homes (if they need care). They do the informal, unpaid day care work of siblings and of parents and of other vulnerable people in families. And all of that is built around the assumption that women are naturally caring. Women are no more naturally caring than men are, but it is a cultural assumption that women will do the work. They are morally and culturally impelled to do care work in the way men are not. Because of this, many women can't enter the public domain to the same degree as men; they can't work late; they can't go out and study at night; they can't go abroad for work; they can't do an awful lot of things if most of the care responsibility is left with them. So, I think there is a big gender equality issue there around care work for Black and White women.

If you want to have Black Irish women in jobs that befit their qualifications, you need targets. Currently, many Black Irish women are in jobs for which they are overqualified. I think we need to say, 'Right, what can they offer and how can we give these women an opportunity to offer something new, to advance'. Inclusion is about enabling people to fulfil themselves; it is not just a matter of having the face of a Black Irish woman on a poster or on the front page of the website. That is meaningless.

14.4 We need a national plan and a higher education fund to create a culturally rich and diverse university

We urgently need a national plan to include minorities from underrepresented backgrounds in the labour force, particularly those who are Black or Brown and living in Ireland already. The universities hire many people from other countries, mostly White people, so we do have minorities, but they are relatively speaking privileged minorities who hold academic posts, and they are overwhelmingly White.

I am going to talk about the Black Irish people who are living in Ireland who are well qualified and who have been here for a long time. I think there is a need to have an action plan, and a national higher education fund, to actually create a culturally rich and diverse university.

If we are to be truly inclusive in employment terms, we have to give minorities jobs that fit their qualifications and endure we have systems in place to recognise their prior qualifications. It is not just about having Black or minority women or men in some lower-end, temporary posts where they will actually have no power, no influence, or anything else. So, I definitely feel we need a national action plan to see real change.

There is a wider problem as we all know, the colonised curriculum. The fact that our knowledge itself is so Western and White. You look at the references that most people have on their reading list, the books that they recommend, they are almost entirely White and Western. Yet, there are many scholars who are not from these cultures. But we don't read them and this is a particular problem in universities in Anglophone countries. We tend to read British, American, Australian and Canadian scholars' work, or work translated into English. This is a very big issue as well; what do we teach the students? What do we allow/enable students to read? What are they allowed to know? What is kept silent?

Given the high levels of colour-based racism in Ireland, Black Studies should be available in the university. And, not just in one university. It should be in many but it needs to be a proper subject where people are employed to teach it, not just on a part-time basis, because that is not sustainable. It is not sustainable for the students, for the university or the person. So, we need to have a different vision of what a university is now, in terms of staffing and curricula. We are still operating with a model of the university that comes from a Eurocentric era. It is not really appropriate for the highly diverse cultures that we have within Ireland. There also needs to be targets set for employing Black people in Irish universities; there are many academically well-qualified Black Irish women and men in different fields, but they are not being hired. We know already that it has taken several generations for a tiny number of Travellers to get employment as academics in Ireland. The same will happen for those who are Black if there is no plan.

We need to ask awkward questions: is it right to have only White people teaching about Black issues of colonisation etc.? Should men run gender inequality programmes focused on women? I'm not saying that men can't talk about gender but if you are talking about inequality experienced by women then a lot of people would feel that women know a lot more about this. So maybe start with women as they have both experiential knowledge academic knowledge. The same applies to issues like colour-based racism. I think a lot of the time those of us who are White don't understand racism. We have never been stopped or brought aside in the airport because of the colour of our skin. We have never been queried going into a shop, or looked at or passed over, as I experienced with Ebun Joseph one time at a restaurant. The person behind the counter took my order before hers although she was ahead of me. That is an unbelievable, degrading, racist experience, an experience White people do not know. And I think that White people never have that experience. That is why we need to learn from those who know what racism is, at micro levels as well as macro levels. We need to understand the colonised world that we live in and the continued colonisation of the world.

What so depressed me, the few times I have been in different African countries, is that everything is taught through English, especially in the universities. The local language, the local culture is totally disrespected. And people are told that it is good for them. What do you learn from this action? You learn that your culture doesn't matter. You learn that your language doesn't matter. I think that the problem that Ireland has is a global problem in relation to colonisation and Eurocentrism; both are so much part of our cultural tradition.

I would hope I would see a lot more Black scholars in Irish universities, full time, permanently engaged, not just in Black Studies because they could have scientific and other academic interests, literature interests, which have nothing to do with racism per se.

We urgently need to decolonise our curricula in racial and ethnic terms, in disability and social class terms as well. The staff in most universities are overwhelmingly middle class; Ireland has very, very few people who come out and self-identify as working class who are academics because we haven't encouraged or enabled them to enter, or if they enter, to come out and speak about class. If they do come from working class backgrounds they learn to pass as middle class. Now if you are Black you can't learn to pass as White, as colour can't be concealed; but if you are working class or a Traveller, it is a big issue. People don't want to self-identify, not just in the universities, but in other areas of employment for fear of discrimination.

Universities and employers generally often advertise the one or two people who have succeeded against all odds, and we say: Look, here is a Black woman or a Traveller who has 'made it'. This is dangerous as it creates an illusion that the selection of the few will become the pattern of the many. That is not possible, as the system of selection is not designed to achieve this. We need robust plans for encouraging minorities into the universities (and other fields of high-status employment) with targets, timeframes, and sanctions, not tokenism.

Ireland is a class-divided society as well as an ethnic and a racially divided one. There are many brilliant scholars and organic intellectuals working, not just in working class communities, but in other ethnic minority communities, who have a lot to teach us within the universities. I think that we should be liaising much more with these embedded organic intellectuals. They have a lot to teach those who are traditional intellectuals in the university.

Kathleen Lynch
Professor of Equality Studies

References

Connell, R. W. 1995. *Masculinities*. Cambridge: Polity Press.

Connell, R. W. and Wood, J. 2005. Globalization and business masculinities. *Men and Masculinities*, 7 (4): 347-64.

Kwesi Tsri, K. 2015. Africans are not Black: why the use of the term 'Black' for Africans should be abandoned Pages 147-160 |
https://doi.org/10.1080/14725843.2015.1113120

Lister, R. 2003. *Citizenship: Feminist Perspectives*. Basingstoke: Palgrave Macmillan.

Lynch, K. 2022. *Care and Capitalism: Why Affective Equality Matters for Social Justice*. Cambridge: Polity Press.

Patel, R. and Moore, J. W. 2018. *A History of the World in Seven Cheap Things: A Guide to Capitalism, Nature and the Future of the Planet*. New York: Verso

https://www.cso.ie/en/releasesandpublications/er/eampb/employmentanalysisofmaternityandpaternitybenefits2016-2019/ Most of those who do not get a top up on maternity benefit have wages below the benefit level of €250 per week.

15

Seeing the human as the human is not as we want them to be

Dr. Mel Duffy
Lecturer, Sociology and Sexuality Studies
Dublin City University

15.1 Introduction

Equity for all women is recognising each and every one as they present themselves to us. It is seeing the human as the human is, not as the human we want them to be. It is also about acknowledging and embracing what each individual presents and brings to different situations. We cannot expect every woman to be or act exactly the same way, neither can we expect all women to be at the same intellectual level. In my case for example, what I am good at is sociology, lecturing, and writing about it. But I would be dreadful running a shop, being in a business, or other such ventures because these are examples of the things I just naturally cannot do because I have no inclination towards them. This doesn't mean that if I am presenting differently at work that there is something inherently wrong with me. It means my skill set, my ways of thinking, my way of being allows me to move into spaces that are comfortable for me or I can navigate those spaces without concern. However, those spaces in themselves do not present themselves to all women and this becomes inherently difficult. If I am a woman with an intellectual disability, I am immediately removed from the whole environment of work, per se, or I might be put into work environments that are considered to be less demanding. We apply work to various levels that humans present themselves as or we hold a set of assumptions about the work that people can or cannot undertake. These sets of assumptions are either correct or incorrect but are rarely interrogated.

15.2 How certain gender stereotypes became solidified in Ireland

If we look at what has been happening in Irish society, from my perspective growing up in Ireland, people who were seen as different, for example people with intellectual disabilities, were removed from society and put into institutions. Women who were pregnant outside of marriage were removed from society and put into institutions. Ireland created a society that presented ableness to a large extent but an ableness that centred on the ability to adhere to the norms and values and belief systems of the time. At that time, if you had a child outside marriage, somehow you were seen as a 'fallen' woman. Whatever does that mean? It however also means it lets the men off the hook as it is centred on the women. A lot of the continuation of the values of society ends up falling to women. For example, women continued the attendance at church (or 'mass' as it is termed in Ireland) because they brought the children to church, men didn't per se. Women were removed from the labour force when they got married up until 1973 prior to Ireland entering the European Economic Community in 1973. Upon marriage, Irish women could not work outside the home. Their primary role in society was the rearing of children, and this nurturing and rearing of their children was for the maintenance of the status quo. The woman was responsible for the creation of the good citizens of the future. Plato talked about men being for the world and women didn't exist. We had this notion of the private and public spheres. Who does this public realm belong to? Who can walk through the public realm? Although Irish women were not allowed to work outside the home, they still had to carry out the cleaning of offices which was done by women from lower socio-economic groupings. These kinds of actions sent messages to boys and girls about what should happen within society.

15.3 Responding or reacting to difference in Ireland

The Irish have a tradition of always going abroad. As a migrant and immigration society, we move naturally in and out of societies. We often don't think about whether we need a passport – we do. We don't think about being White and that there's going to be difficulties when we land somewhere. We have celebrations like St. Patrick's Day coming up, and we embrace the notion of various parts of the world turning green representing who the Irish are and we embrace that. We have a Taoiseach who will go to Washington to talk to the US President. This happens on the 17th of March every year, (bar Covid times), Ireland's Taoiseach will be talking to the American President. That is power. And it is taken for granted that we can move through these societies with ease without questioning. However, when the difference presents itself to Ireland, we don't know how to handle it. Kathleen Lynch's early work illustrated how we created segregation within our society. Ireland had girls' schools, and boys' schools. Once you start creating segregation, you teach difference. This separationism creates the inability to move smoothly within differences, because you are separating by keeping groups and categories separate. Just like we base this separation on gender, we also base it on religion. We may have Catholic schools, and non-Catholic schools, and we may have Protestant schools. In essence, Ireland does not deal with differences well. This is particularly problematic when we start moving into having a multicultural society. If we create areas that are 'Black only' 'Indian only' 'French only' 'Brazilian only' because there are many ethnicities within Ireland, we are in danger of creating racialised ghettos.

15.4 Question what is so great about you that others must be expected to be like you?

We are required to move and live beside each other and learn about and from each other. We can learn that each culture brings with it and to us challenges, and indeed gifts in ways of thinking and ways of doing that make us think about how we do things. It can also challenge us to change and embrace new ways of knowing. We should ideally be open to answering the question: why are my ways right or why do I think my ways are right? For example, we have norms in relation to family but when I create my own family, I can do within my family what suits my family. I create with the people in my family norms, and because the norms are developed and created by us, they are not immoveable or cast in stone. My brothers will do it differently within their families. My sister will do it differently within their families and we meet and our families are different. But because they are your brother or sister, you embrace the difference because theoretically, we like each other. But if we put people in who are categorised as different, then we begin to ask questions. I'll give an example. I happen to be a lesbian, and I knew how to traverse the heterosexual world. But over time, I no longer do that. I am me. I travel as a lesbian woman within the heterosexual world. It has meant meeting the Berlin walls every now and then. You have to decide whether you are climbing the wall or you are taking one brick at a time out so that you can get through the wall. However, if you are a Black person, you can't pass as White within Irish society or the Western world. Because unlike me, who *can* choose to pass as straight, if you are Black or Brown, you can't choose to be White. It is often like saying to people, if you want to live with me, be like me. We forget to question what is so great about me that others must be expected to be like me. This puts people in a power position. We are not all the same, we are different and being different is good for us. It is good for society; it is good for Ireland.

15.5. What do we need for Black women to have equity
Acceptance of everyday and ordinary people

We have to first of all recognize that Black Irish women are Irish. Being Irish does not equate being White. We have a whole history of Irish who are not White. We have seen it with diverse examples, with Paul McGrath, one of Ireland's great Irish soccer players embraced by and in Ireland. Ever wondered why? Was it because he did things that brought greatness to the country. We have another great Irish athlete at the moment who happens to be Black and Irish and we adore her. Why? Because she is going to do and bring to Ireland a sense of greatness in athleticism etc and the majority of the Irish embrace that. The implication is that we are only going to embrace those who bring accolades to Ireland. The question then arises, if we are going to embrace those who are ordinary, everyday people like you and I, and how do we do this in the world of work?

Recognition of qualification and difference in recruitment

We need to create the spaces at interviews that recognizes differences and show that the company acknowledges and respects these differences. If we don't do that, then we are clearly stating that this is not the world of work for you. Equally, we must be very good at recognising the qualifications of those who come from countries of origin outside Europe. In other words, a qualification from a country of people with white skin does not mean it is better. Neither does a European qualification mean it is better. It is equal and it is recognising the diversity and the equality of the education and the brilliance of the education that is in the African Nations. In a lot of ways, we don't. I remember working as a care assistant in a hospice in London at one stage in my life. Many of the women I worked with were women of African descent. Many of them could not get their qualifications in nursing recognized, yet they came from post-colonial British colonies and their education wasn't recognized. This is despite some of those institutions being set up by the British Empire in those countries. This gives an indication about the type of education that is accepted.

Remove roadblocks and ensure representation at all levels

We need to make sure we are not putting road blocks for moving up the chain within workplaces ensuring that movement up the food chain and promotional aspects are equally available as they are for a White person. The other aspect starts in the classroom. Take for example, a 4-year-old born in Ireland to parents of African descent from Nigeria or maybe Ethiopia. As it is in Ireland today, the only time they will see a person like themselves teaching is at home. How can they develop to their full potential? I don't want to be that 'exotic' child for want of a better word. I would need to see representations of me in the classroom. Sometimes, you need to see if it's the SNA or the teacher. This way, they can aspire and be their best self and all of themselves. There's a reason Kamala Harris, when she became the vice president of America said, now young girls and young women can see that there are women like me in positions of power. That's what we need to see. We need to see that representation so that young girls can dream. Young girls can see women in positions, whether it is in gynaecology, law, astronaut, industry leadership, or third level education.

15.6. Only Black Irish women truly know what it's like to be a Black woman in Ireland

For our female politicians, it is very difficult at the moment in relation to the amount of online abuse they are getting. Imagine what it would be like for a Black woman. Would it be doubled down or more? We however don't ask Black women what it is like to be in Irish society. How do you move through Irish society? Such a study has to be done by Black women because I don't know Black women, I don't know what it is like to be a Black woman but I can tell you what it is like being a lesbian woman within society and I can tell you how it has changed or maybe at times I think it has changed and then I find that it hasn't changed. We need to see representation of the self in leadership positions so that we can be inspired to emulate this. And in art as well and theatre and all of these spaces, the same thing applies, 'if you see it, you can become it'. If you don't see it, then you don't see a space for yourself.

15.7 How do we meet the person that is categorised as Black

Ireland will change whether it wants to or not. It will take a while, but we are not the enemy, they are not the enemy. It is like saying when you have a group of men who happen to be living in a certain area that people begin to fear mongering about them being dangerous. But we have had groups of men living in areas for years, but they were called priests and nobody feared them, but they were White. Why is it if your skin is a different colour, we perceive it somehow as a negative. How do we meet the person that is categorised as Black? I went to college in Maynooth as an undergraduate. There was a great Sociologist there called Fr. Micheal Mac Greil. He was a Jesuit, and I remember one day calling him Father. He turned around to me and he said, 'I'm not Father' (because that is what we called priests at the time), and he said 'you have one father so I am not father. I am a priest so you can call me Dr. Mac Greil'. But one of the things that he did was really, really interesting. Back in the 1980s when I was there, he carried out a survey every year of the students and looked at the student's profile and the integration between the Black and White students and he asked questions like, do you take them home? do you go for coffee with them? would you go for a drink with them, would you bring a Black person home with you for dinner in the same way as you would bring a White friend home for dinner?

When you come from the position of the other as being equal to you, you will discover how we can understand each other and ask questions. From my perspective, I worked with this wonderful Ghanian woman when I was in London in the hospice. I learnt from her that asking questions is not wrong as it leads to understanding. She facilitated my curiosity and understanding of being different. Don't be afraid of asking questions because you will learn from the answers that there is not that much difference between us as we love the same, we may dislike the same basically we are trying to go through life living each day as it comes.

15.8 Embracing is a mindset; embrace each other

It is important that we embrace each other. Embracing is a mindset. Are you willing to go that distance to know that person? Are you willing to work with that person? It is not a case of what can you do for the image of my company, rather what can my company do to embrace a diverse Ireland which is new and developing. In some ways, it is not that new, people are here 20–30+ years, they should not still be feeling like outsiders at this stage. They should feel that they and their next generations are as Irish as my children are. I think the workplace may help to change that. Because we have to change, we have no choice, but we shouldn't see it as a negative. We should see it as we are making the choice to change and if we do change, we can create in society what we don't even know could exist. Many are afraid of what they don't know but as an academic, I love what I don't know and not knowing something is where you start chip, chip, chipping away and I think if we start chip, chip, chipping away at each other to learn from each other we would realise that we can create things together that we've never thought was possible or could exist.

Dr Mel Duffy

16

Accepting, valuing and supporting Black Irish women in place- making in Ireland

Dr Ebun Joseph, CEO & founder, Institute of Anti-racism and Black Studies
Professor Emerita Kathleen Lynch, UCD Equality Studies
Senator Tom Clonan, Member of Seanad Éireann

16.1 Introduction

Do Black Irish women truly experience equity in the labour market in Ireland? In this book, we were confronted with the stark reality that Black Irish women face notable disparities. If you read the section in each chapter of the pathways of the authors, you would have read so many self-reported stories of retraining 3-5 academic levels lower than their highest academic qualification. For example, someone with a Master's degree which is a level 9 in Ireland, retraining to a level 5 course in order to access employment. The cost of equity for the Black Irish woman is high. Not just for the Black Irish woman who experience a brain waste by being [un]underemployed, but it is also a brain waste for Ireland as the receiving nation and the countries from which they arrived in Ireland, it is a brain drain.

For the Black Irish woman, it is a constant battle to prove oneself, to overcome barriers that others do not face. The time, effort, and emotional toll it takes to navigate the labour market as a person of African descent in Ireland is immense. The constant cycle of retraining, volunteering, and being told you are not good enough can be disheartening. It is a system that seems to be stacked against you from the start. But despite all of this, there is resilience. There is a determination to keep pushing forward, to keep fighting for a place at the table. The Black Irish woman continues to strive for success, to prove that she is just as capable as anyone else. And while the cost of equity may be high, the hope for a better future, for a more equitable society, keeps her going.

16.2 Forging positive visibility for Black Irish women - Senator Tom Clonan

The experiences of professional Black Irish women in Ireland as explored in the documentary that has inspired this book really opened my eyes to gendered and raced inequality in the Republic of Ireland.

A number of things struck me very forcefully about the documentary – and about the publication of this book. I am a middle-aged White Irishman, an academic, journalist, and politician. As a younger man in my twenties, I was an  army officer (Captain) in Ireland's armed forces. In that capacity, I completed a PhD while working as a serving officer which explored the experiences of my female colleagues of military service in Ireland. The research uncovered shockingly high levels of gender-based discrimination, gender-based bullying, sexual harassment and gender-based violence up to and including sexual assault and rape.

As a male officer, I had never been bullied, harassed, or sexually assaulted. As a young man who was fully immersed in the values and norms of a hyper-masculine military workplace – I had no insight into the experiences of my female colleagues. It was only through the collaborative approach of research – informed by a feminist methodology and rooted in the literature on workplace equality – that I developed an awareness of the negative experiences of my sisters in arms. The publication of my PhD thesis in 2000 kick-started a long and painful process which has culminated in 2024 with a full Judicial Enquiry into the culture of Ireland's armed forces. Hopefully this will lead to the transformation required to bring our military into the 21st century with regard to dignity, diversity, and equity in the armed forces of this country. Watching the documentary on the experiences of professional Black Irish women generated the same 'culture shock' I had experienced as a young army officer researching the experiences of my female comrades. It powerfully communicated to me – as a privileged White male - the embedded patterns of disadvantage, hostile scrutiny, power inequality, and intersectional discrimination experienced by female emigrants and Irish-born women from ethnic minorities.

For me, this has been an inflection point and I cannot emphasise how important it is to me – as an Irish citizen and feminist – that we support the positive visibility and advocacy of the authors of this book. Ireland is in sore need of a broadening of Black studies and a robust ethical assessment of the powerful patterns of intersectional discrimination – along gendered and raced lines – that exist in the Irish Republic. My experience as a researcher of such injustice – with all of the life-limiting and life-altering implications for Irish soldiers, sailors and air-crew – was a microcosm of sorts of the wider societal experiences of Black Irish women and migrant women in Ireland.

I am confident that the work of the authors of this book – and this exercise in forging positive visibility – will lead to the changes in Irish society that are necessary to combat gendered and raced discrimination. For me it is an awakening. I believe that Dr. Joseph and all of the women who have contributed to this work have started the process of transformation which is necessary in Irish social, cultural, educational, and economic life. It is a timely intervention.

16.3 Stories of well-educated Black Irish women within a White wall - Kathleen Lynch UCD

Having read the stories of discrimination and profound disrespect experienced by so many Black Irish women in this book, I am lost for words. What is most disturbing is that the women who are telling their stories are

well-educated, all have third-level qualifications, some have more than 1 postgraduate qualifications, and many are senior professionals in their field. Yet, they are treated as second-class citizens, disrespected, and disregarded, simply because of their skin colour, while their gender further exacerbates their experience of discrimination at work. What is striking too is that, to recover their self-respect, the women spoke at length at how exhausting it was emotionally, not only to process daily petty and not so petty discriminations, but to try to support family and community members experiencing insults and harms.

Ebun's own published research showed that people of Black African descent, even when they had relevant qualifications and experience, and spoke English fluently, had to wait for long periods, sometimes up to 2 years, to get a job as a volunteer! This led them into a highly expensive and demoralising cycle of continually retraining and volunteering in the hope of securing a job. The stories of Black women in Ireland who are not educated and articulate would undoubtedly be even worse.

Facing a White wall

Predominantly White societies like Ireland, have to do major educational, cultural, political, and ideological work to create a cultural milieu where Black women are treated equally to White women and men. It will be a long journey, not least because almost all of those who occupy positions of power in politics, in cultural, educational and other work organisations are overwhelmingly White. As one of the persons recounted to Ebun, in the counter-story outlined in the opening chapter, even if you get a job and then experience racism at work, the CEO is White, the HR manager is White, the line manager is White and your colleagues are White. In making a complaint or challenging a racial injustice, one faces a wall of White power that appears impregnable, even if it is not. As the woman who experienced discrimination noted, raising a race-related discrimination in a 'room' of White people is like asking a female rape victim to report their rape to roomful of men. It does not and will not work, not least because the White 'room' has no experiential knowledge of this type of experience, and because claims of colour-based racial discrimination are a challenge to the White privilege that they enjoy, a 'White' dividend, of which most White people are completely unaware.

Action plans

To break down the White-male wall, work organisations (including educational organisations, such as schools, colleges, curriculum bodies and teacher unions), need to develop a plan to have Black women employed, supported, educated, and promoted to key decision-making positions in their areas of employment. There has to be an Racial Equality Action Plan that is both credible and coherent. There must be targets, timeframes, strategies (and sanctions for failure), if any Action Plan is to be meaningfully implemented.

'Nothing about us without us'

Black women must be at the table where power is exercised if they are to determine the conditions of employment and opportunity for other Black women. The principle of 'Nothing about Us, without Us', which underpins the call by people with disabilities to be respected in decision-making, also applies to Black people (and other minorities, including Travellers, Roma) in a predominantly White society.

Reflexivity

There is also a need to develop a Culture of Organisational Reflexivity and Self Reflexivity about equality practices in work organisations. This is not about having online or written policies promising equal opportunity principles. These types of policies are generally never read and are frequently ignored in practice. What is needed is developing a culture of inner self-appraisal, inner to the person and inner to the work organisation. Operationalising racial and gender reflexivity (ideally reflexivity on all equality grounds) should become part of the organisation's strategic plan, and part of performance appraisal both for oneself and for others on an ongoing basis. We could start with the question: What have I/we done this year to promote racial equality for Black women at work?

Working for nothing!

What is striking about the interviews is that many women reported being expected to work for nothing. To volunteer to help others in one's spare time is indeed a valuable thing to do. However, many highly skilled Black women, without employment, were expected to volunteer without compensation for long periods. They were invited to 'advise' on racial policies or give 'talks' about anti-racism without remuneration. Invitations of this type came from people who were employed. Perhaps these interviews will call attention to the deep disrespect involved in asking people to 'volunteer' to work for nothing, when they need remuneration, and especially when there is no possible opportunity for employment following the volunteering.

16.4 Acceptance of Black and African Irish women
- Ebun Joseph

The routine lack of acceptance of Black Irish women through persistent devaluation of their qualifications, skills, competences, capacities, and personality perpetuates their underrepresentation in the workforce and is the bedrock of the inequity seen in the Irish labour market today. The hurdles faced by Black Irish women in accessing equity is because of their intersectionality (overlapping social identities in relation to). This is not just about women as the victims of misogyny or racism; it's the interaction of both gender and race that compounds the difficulties for them. The complicated layers of discrimination they deal with demand a nuanced approach to dismantling those barriers.

To illustrate the concept of how complex it really is I have created two stories. Story A, is commonly told by organisations who feel they are doing very well in achieving EDI, but their Black staff are still experiencing racism reflected in a higher staff turnover than other groups. Story B tells the counter story that shows the side that many organisations do not always see.

Story A:
A line manager talking with members of her senior management team (SMT) after they won an award for excellence in EDI (equality, diversity and inclusion) for the past 3rd years in a row.

SMT: Congratulations on this latest EDI award! We are doing really well with inclusion and diversity. Our numbers of people from diverse groups are increasing.

Manager: Thank you. It also helps that we now have a budget to work with and we have a small team. We are able to complete the tasks and monitor the progress.

SMT: What were the key things that caused this shift? Five years ago, we didn't have any staff members who were born outside Europe.

Manager: We invested in staff training. We offered a 1-hour unconscious bias training to staff members. We also recruited interns from diverse background. This helped boost our numbers. We have also set up an employee relations group (ERG). We celebrate some key dates for different groups and we try to get some understanding of different cultures by having a taste of food from different parts of the world on offer in the canteen.

SMT: It's great to see the numbers increasing. Any challenge with the increased numbers of diverse staff?

Manager: They are settling in okay. We are working to make sure they have a sense of belonging in the organisation. We have our equality statement on the website and at different locations around the office. We also make sure new hires are aware of our equality statement.

SMT: At the last training session, I was in briefly with your team, and some staff members mentioned the fear of saying the wrong thing when in diverse groups. Some talked about not knowing how to address a person who is not White. They were worried about causing offence. How is that working out?

Manager: No, it is going well. There's more interaction. Although we lost two of our Black staff members recently. One actually decided to leave on her own. She said she got another job. The second one, we had to ask her to leave as we noticed her speed was going to be a problem. She did not meet her target for the month. And it was easier to ask her to leave at the beginning than wait until it became a real problem. We are keen to ensure that bringing people of diverse backgrounds in is not going to cause a problem for organisational output or reduce the standard of our work.

***

Counter story B: A line manager talking to a Black Irish woman (BIW) after her organisation just won an award for EDI excellence

Manager: How would you rate this organisation in terms of your sense of belonging? Do you feel you belong here?

BIW: Is this a trick question or are you genuinely looking for answers?

Manager: I want to know. It will help us know how to keep improving our work.

BIW: Okay. How can I belong to a place where I am not accepted? How would that work?

Manager: Well, we have done some EDI training and many of the experts are talking about belonging and meeting the belonging needs of our staff. I want to know what we can do to help you feel more like you belong here.

BIW: I think the argument is faulty from the beginning. If you want to help me belong, then you have to accept me as a person of equal status, and rights as an equal human being to yourself. Think about it…, if the organisation's focus is on me belonging, helping me to feel like I belong, then you have made *me* the problem. That whole process positions me as a problem that needs to be fixed. It locates the variable and problem in me. That's the problem we constantly have where I as symbolic of the Black person is positioned as the problem.

Manager: Okay. Then what do you want if not to belong?

BIW: I want to belong, but being accepted is what helps me to belong. That means you won't be looking for the changes and adjustments to come from me, the only new individual who has come to your organisation, who does not even have the power to influence anything to make the adjustment. If we focus on acceptance, then the organisation will need to examine its processes how it operates that would show that you accept me as an equal person.

Manager: We have done a number of things, like marking out your cultural dates on the calendar, sharing your food, and bringing in speakers to share their experiences.

BIW: Yes, but most of the time, you expect people who come to give the talks to use emotional labour. You expect their passion to change the outcomes for their community to be the fee you pay them. Even when you pay them, you literally pay them peanuts. The ERG with the lowest budget is the one that is for race or for Black groups. And we need to have sandwiches and coffee for these events, the same is provided for all other events Don't get me wrong, the speakers you have had have been good and hearing of their experience of difference is great, but it doesn't really change things for me. Racism is systemic. Our lives and experience are real, not a Netflix show.

Manager: We have also recruited people who are not White. We recruited you and other staff members, and you are good at your job.

BIW: Yes, and I really appreciate that because it's taken me 2 years to get this role. However, do you know I am massively underemployed? I am training my team members but I was recruited at entry level and so were the other two staff. We don't have power and we can't make any changes. Our presence is still pitched at the very bottom of the ladder. Unless you are recruiting at middle-management level, our presence here does not impact the organisation. I know you won't like this. Ireland prefers us when we can only focus on what is good, tell half-truths about our experiences, and how we are treated.

Manager: Okay, I don't know what to say.

BIW: Let me ask you a question then. If I came to your house to visit you, can I just come in and belong in your house first or would you need to accept me in, welcome me, show me around, and be willing to share the space, resources and power with me? Let's talk about the *misrecognition* of Black people and their credentials from outside the Global North. What this means is that you do not accept us, not that we do not belong.

Manager: It makes sense when you put it like that.

BIW: Belonging is a result of being accepted. We have to be accepted first, then we will belong.

***

It is not that Black Irish women *do not belong* in Ireland or in the workplace, they are just *not accepted as equal* to White women. A Black woman is viewed and evaluated as *less than* a White person. What this means is that skin colour trumps qualifications, skills, competencies, and abilities. In fact, the same value or lack of value, disrespect, and disregard for the Black Irish woman is attributed to their skills, competencies, and capabilities. Older Irish people will remember when money collected in Trócaire boxes in Irish homes were for 'feeding the Black babies' and while the message may have changed, the negative stereotype of Black people unable to look after themselves persists. Then we have had many people coming into Ireland seeking asylum in recent years. Black people are seen through these defective lenses where it is either slavery, or trauma and grinding poverty or a mixture of the colonial past and racist present.

Black women face many microaggressions. When Black women speak up for themselves, they are seen as aggressive or overly confident. They are four times more likely to die during child birth than White women in the UK. And they experience domestic violence at rates higher than any other race. Black women are more likely to change their hair in the workplace to fit in to the social norms because of discrimination in the workplace. Black girls are disproportionately disciplined at school compared to their White peers. They are more likely to face exclusion and expulsion. Black women are one of the fastest growing entrepreneurs in the world; they were also instrumental in many inventions that paved the way for how we live today. What else are we losing and missing by keeping Black Irish women out of the labour market?

The women who contributed to this book have clearly told us what can be done to change their outcomes and make them feel truly accepted and that they belong in Ireland. Please listen to them.

What we need to do:

Accept – Black people as equal citizens *as they are*

Activate – a national programme of quotas and affirmative action across the public sector including schools and in local and national politics

Amplify not Interpret – Do not use your voice to interpret what they say

Support – provide grants for Black women entrepreneurs, run a CO competition in the Irish Civil Service for Black women

Educate – teach Black history & include anti-racism training at all school levels

Healing spaces – provide safe spaces for Black women e.g. where they can safely reflect on their experience of racism, discrimination, impact and affect.

Legislate – put policy into action by passing legislation e.g. Anti-Hate legislation

Recruit – at all levels, especially at management levels

Knowledge – increase knowledge about this group in Irish society by providing funding for research that examines Black women's issues

Train – invest in training of Black Irish staff who manage to get jobs and the human resource professional and recruiters

#Add1Add1More Join the campaign – add 1 Black Irish woman to your team; if you already have one, add one more. Imagine what would happen if all businesses, schools and NGOs added 1 Black Irish woman to their team?

In essence, achieving equity for Black Irish women will require a holistic and concerted effort—addressing both workplace and societal factors—to dismantle ingrained biases and provide an environment where qualifications are valued, opportunities are abundant. Black women will then be accepted as equals and no one will be truly left behind.

∙∙